Loving God &
Loving Gays

What's A Christian To Do?

Eric Elder

Cover art by Kaleo Elder.
Editing by Jeanette Smith.
Author photo by Hayley Breanne Photography.

*Special thanks to: Mike Baker, Bridgette Booth, Shelly Busby,
Bruce Felkins, Matt Fogle, Nicki Green, Michele Larsen,
Al Lowry, Joan Moody, Jessica Pastirik, Greg Potzer,
Jim Probst, Sue Roberts, Kent Sanders, Kim Smith,
Jason Sniff, Tim Wilkins, and my precious family.*

Loving God & Loving Gays is part of a series of
inspirational resources produced by Eric Elder
Ministries. To learn more, please visit:
WWW.INSPIRINGBOOKS.COM

ISBN 978-1-931760-82-9

Table Of Contents

Special Note:

About The Study Guides

This book contains a study guide for each chapter to be used for personal reflection or group study.

These guides are interspersed throughout the book after every two chapters to make it convenient for those who would like to study two chapters per week for six weeks (with an optional seventh week for the Conclusion and Afterword).

To learn more about the study guides and how to use them—plus who I believe will benefit the *most* from this book—please see page 20!

Chapter 1:

My Testimony In A Nutshell

———— ◈ ————

In which I share my testimony in 150 words,
including some words to encourage you
to read this book to the very end.

———— ◈ ————

I went into homosexuality in the summer of 1982. I came out of it in the fall of 1984, thanks in large part to a friend who later became my wife.

In the winter of 1987, God broke any remaining power which homosexuality held over me, once and for all, when I put my faith in Christ for everything in my life.

Since then, I've gotten married, had six kids of my own, and enjoyed an off-the-charts sex life with a woman beyond my dreams.

It's been over 30 years since I came out of homosexuality. I've never gone back, and I never plan to. In this book, I'll share why.

Along the way, I'll share some ideas for how you can walk with others through what may be the most important journey of their lives—and how to do so in a truly loving way.

Eric Elder

Chapter 2:

My Testimony In An *Eggshell*

———— ❖ ————

In which I share how talking about
homosexuality is like walking on eggshells,
for me and for others, perhaps including you.

———— ❖ ————

I don't usually start a conversation by talking about homosexuality.
(I don't usually start a book that way, either.) But it seems that more
and more conversations these days eventually turn toward
homosexuality. And that's not necessarily a bad thing.

For me, as someone who has dealt with homosexual attractions for
much of my life, it's actually a good thing. The fact that you picked up a
book like this tells me that you care. It tells me that you're trying to
understand this issue more so you can love those around you more—
people who may have been wrestling with these feelings, perhaps in
silence, for years.

At the same time, I'll admit that when the topic comes up, it still
makes me a little nervous. Not because of what I know or don't know
about the topic, or what I believe or don't believe about it, but because
of what might happen if I say *anything* about the topic one way or
another. It's one of those hair-trigger issues that can send people into
orbit with little more than a word or even a look, however thoughtful
or well-intentioned.

Even while writing this book, after sending an early draft of it to a
handful of friends, one of them was loving everything about the book
until she got to Chapter 12. When she read one of my suggestions for
how to love gays better, she sent me a note saying, "Sorry, but I have to
wholeheartedly disagree with you on this one. I can't continue reading your
book. I'm done and stopping. I wish you the best."

As she was one of my best and most like-minded friends, I was shocked! I called her immediately to talk through the issue.

After several hours of conversations, over a period of several days, she still didn't budge. Although I changed the wording and changed the tone, I stayed true to my original thoughts. She read it again and wrote again, saying, "I'm sorry, Eric. I really tried. I can't continue with your book. I just can't. I'm still upset, and I can't endorse it. Again, I'm really sorry."

There was nothing I could do but pray. So I did.

That night, she called back. "Eric," she said. "I think I need to take to heart what you're saying in that chapter. There's a truth in there that I think God wants me to see."

Thankfully, the situation was fully resolved by the time she read the final edition a few weeks later, which still contained the same thoughts and beliefs, but with some fresh wording and extra insight. She wrote, "Eric, I couldn't wait. I jumped ahead and read Chapter 12. And I'm crying. Crying tears of joy. It's great. Just great. The wording is perfect."

My point is that if these kinds of conversations take place between dear friends and like-minded believers, it's no wonder this issue causes so much tension between strangers and those who are *not* like-minded.

On the other end of the spectrum, however, there are Christians who don't have strong feelings about this issue one way or another. They're simply not sure what to think.

When I shared with a new friend that I had been involved in homosexuality in the past, she shared with me a dilemma that she and many other Christians are facing:

"I have several gay friends," she said. "I find them to be loving, generous, and kind. It's something of a conundrum for Christians on how to act around gays, isn't it?"

She's right. It *is* a conundrum, a puzzle to be solved, and a puzzle which I've been working to solve for many years as well. My hope in writing this book is to share with you some of the solutions I've found to help you leap ahead and get closer to solving this puzzle for yourself.

HANDLE WITH CARE

While homosexuality is a sensitive topic, that doesn't mean we can't talk about it in a sensitive way—a way that truly brings life and hope and encouragement to those around us.

I'm thankful that someone took the time to write down what God had spoken to him about this topic, even though the words he wrote were written nearly 2,000 years ago and over 5,000 miles away from where I lived. Those few words, just a few paragraphs, really, were written to the Christians in Rome by a man named Paul.

When I read those words *30* years ago, they changed my life for good and forever, both here on earth and for eternity. I'll share more of what Paul said and how his words impacted me in Chapter 6. Right now I want you to know that your words are important, too, and your actions equally so.

I want to commend you for picking up this book, for learning all that you can learn, and for wanting to do something to help others in this important area. You never know how one word, one look, or one thoughtful act of love could change someone's life, including your own. (For instance, the friend who helped me the most eventually became my wife. Your results may vary!)

I've shared my story with many people over the past 30 years— hundreds of people in one-on-one conversations and thousands more at conferences and online. Yet every time I talk about homosexuality— every time!—I do so with a fair amount of trepidation.

I used to be afraid of sharing my testimony because of people who *hated* gays. I was afraid of what they might think of me or how they might treat me because of what I had done. (If Kermit the Frog thought it wasn't easy being green, I wonder how he would have felt if people thought he was gay.)

But things have changed so dramatically in the last few years that I'm *still* afraid every time I share my testimony. The difference now is that I'm afraid of people who *love* gays! I'm afraid of what they might think of me or how they might treat me because of what I've shared. I'm afraid they might think, wrongly, that somehow I must hate gays because of what I've shared. The truth is that I love gays now more than when I was gay! The difference now is that I'm able to *truly* love them, not for what I can get from them, but for who they really are.

In spite of my fears, I've found that whenever I do share my testimony, people earnestly respond with great joy. My story seems to increase people's faith that God can do anything—absolutely anything.

People realize that if God could touch my life in such a deep and profound way, then He could do anything for anyone who is living in something in which they don't want to be living.

As much as I fear sharing my testimony, the reason I *keep* sharing it is because it gives hope to so many. God really is in the life-changing business. That's one of His specialties.

Aside from the shift over the years in why I'm afraid of sharing my testimony, I've also noticed a shift in how much people know today regarding this topic—and how much more they *still* want to know.

NUANCES ABOUND

The conversation regarding homosexuality today is much more nuanced than ever before.

When I published a book of my testimony a few years ago, not just in a nutshell, but in a 67,000-word book which detailed how God had changed my thoughts and desires in this area, the response was phenomenal. The comments and questions that I received from the readers of the first 100 copies of that book surpassed the word count of the entire book!

What I thought would be a book that would satisfy readers' desires to know more turned out to be a book that generated still more questions and conversations. People are hungry to know more about this topic.

What I love about this hunger is that I can tell people truly want to understand this issue as best as they can. They truly want to help their friends and family members as much as possible. Since you've read this far, I'm guessing you're in this category, too.

What is difficult about this hunger is that people's questions are so much more nuanced. It's so much harder to give "simple" answers to "simple" questions. The questions *behind* the questions seem almost endless.

There are times when I feel a bit like one of the blind men whom Jesus healed, as recorded in the Bible. His "testimony in a nutshell" goes like this: "I was blind, but now I see."

Some people jumped for joy when they heard the man's story, accepting what he said with great enthusiasm.

Others, however, wanted to know more. Their questions and comments were more nuanced as well. It's as if they wanted to know, "How blind were you, exactly? And how much can you see now?"

It wasn't enough for the man to just *say* that he had been changed. The people wanted to know, in detail, precisely what that change entailed.

Some people wondered if he had really been blind before. They wondered if he was the man he claimed to be or just someone who looked like that man. Still others wanted to prove him wrong no matter what he said, either dismissing him completely or dismissing the one to whom he had given credit for healing him.

To all this, he simply replied: "One thing I do know. I was blind, but now I see!" (John 9:25b).

For me, it's okay if people ask me questions. I don't mind answering them.

When people ask how "blind" I was before, in my case meaning, "How strong were your attractions for men in the past?" I don't mind telling them that they were very strong. I think it's important for people to hear.

When people ask if I could "see" at all before, in my case meaning, "Were you ever attracted to women in the past?" I'm okay with telling them that I was—but that I had never been sexually intimate with a woman until I met the woman who became my wife.

When people ask how much I can "see" now, I don't mind telling them that I had an off-the-charts sexual relationship with my wife for over 23 years, until I lost her to cancer in 2012.

And when people ask if I have changed completely, no longer having *any* attractions to men, I don't mind telling them that I do still have occasional thoughts and desires in that direction—but that the power that those thoughts and desires once held over my life has been broken. Any gay thoughts I still have no longer control me or my actions like they did before.

People *want* to know these things, and I don't mind telling them, even if their motives are, perhaps, to simply find fault with whatever I'm saying. As David Swift wrote in his script for the movie *Pollyanna:* "If you're looking for the bad in someone, expecting to find it, you certainly will."

If someone were to look for a flaw in me or in my story to which they could point as support for their position, no matter what it might be, then I'm sure they could find something. But if someone is asking a question, I don't mind answering that person, either, as I believe it's important to get all the facts on the table.

I'm still amazed every time I hear about a split decision in the U.S. Supreme Court. I'm amazed because the court is comprised of nine of the smartest people in our country who are looking at the exact same set of facts, yet the judges often come to completely opposite conclusions. The final vote is frequently 5-4 or 4-5 in any given case.

Why? It's not the facts so much that lead to these different conclusions, but what people bring to those facts, what they've learned outside of them, or what they're trying to achieve when interpreting those facts.

BLIND SPOTS

I don't fault people for having different opinions on what they may or may not see in my story. In the marketplace of ideas, I believe mine will hold up as strongly as, if not stronger than, any others.

And like the blind man who was healed by Jesus, I know what God has done for me. Like the blind man, the one thing I *do* know is this: "I was blind, but now I see!"

So if someone is reading this book and looking for reasons to discount what I'm saying, I don't mind. But I hope they won't be like the man in a fictional story who thought he was dead and went to a psychiatrist to confirm his belief that he was, in fact, dead.

After telling his psychiatrist that he thought he was dead, the psychiatrist asked him, "Do dead men bleed?"

The man thought about the psychiatrist's question and, realizing that when a man dies, his heart stops pumping and his blood stops flowing, he responded, "No, dead men don't bleed."

The psychiatrist then asked him to take a pin and prick his finger to see if it would bleed or not. The man did so, and blood started spurting from his finger. The man exclaimed, "What do you know? Dead men *do* bleed!"

Some people are convinced of their opinions no matter what evidence is presented to the contrary. If that's you, then I doubt there is anything I could say that will convince you otherwise.

But if you're like I was when I was delving into this subject to find out what God really thought and felt and wanted for me in this area of my life—and I was willing to accept whatever I found as the truth, because I knew that whatever *God* wanted for me would be *better* than whatever I might have wanted for myself—then this will be a very worthwhile endeavor.

We all have spiritual blind spots, myself included, and without asking God to reveal them to us through His Holy Spirit, we simply cannot see them on our own. I have been asking God to reveal mine to me ever since I put my faith in Christ, and I have been continually amazed at the results.

GOING ALL THE WAY

To those who love gays and want to support and encourage them as much as possible, let me say this: "Thank you!" There has never in my lifetime been more interest in this topic than there is now, whether in our country or in our world. From the President on down, this topic continues to attract national and international attention.

While some people may feel uncomfortable with the amount of attention being given to this subject, I am personally very thankful that so many people are willing to take a look, many for the very first time, at the tremendous pressures, struggles, and heartaches faced by those with same-sex attractions.

In many ways, I wish I had seen such a great groundswell of people seeking to understand this issue 30 and 40 years ago when I was first wrestling through all of these questions so deeply, seemingly all alone.

On behalf of myself and others who have ever had feelings of attraction toward those of their same sex, I truly want to say, "Thank you." Thank you for your willingness to learn, to understand, and to try to be as loving as possible toward those for whom this subject is a daily reality.

I also want to encourage you to *go all the way in your love for others*, not stopping short when you find one or two nuggets of truth. I want you to keep asking and keep seeking greater understanding so you can offer something of exceedingly great value to those you love.

There is a natural life cycle through which people go whenever they're learning about a topic that is new to them. Sometimes people call off the search too quickly, having found *some* nuggets of truth, but *not anywhere near* the whole truth.

I've been exploring this subject for over 30 years, and I can tell you about my own life cycle of learning on this issue. Many of the steps took *years*.

It took *years* for me to go from fearing other people when they called me gay, to wondering what was so wrong with being gay anyway, to accepting those who engaged in it, to finally diving into homosexuality myself. It also took *years* before I realized the long-term impact of what I was doing, how it was shortchanging me from the fullness of what *God* wanted for my life (and what I, in fact, wanted for my life), and how it was actually destructive to me and to those around me.

It took years for me to realize that being gay was not just one of several options regarding my sexuality, or the second-best option, but that it could have truly destroyed me if I had stayed on that path.

I didn't go into homosexuality overnight, and I didn't come out of it overnight, either, even though my decision to leave it for good came in one fell swoop when I put my faith in Christ for everything in my life, including my sexuality. That's when I felt like the psalmist who wrote: "I run in the path of Your commands, for You have set my heart free" (Psalm 119:32).

I don't know where you are on the life cycle of learning about this issue. You may have been thinking and praying about this subject for quite some time, and maybe you've come to some conclusions about it so far.

But if those conclusions don't fit with what you know from nature, from the way God has designed people and plants and animals to use their sexual organs; and if those conclusions don't fit with what you know from the Bible, in which God has given us some of the most strongly worded warnings about this and other topics to keep us from harm; then let me encourage you to keep asking, keep seeking, and keep knocking until you find something that *is* in line with what you see in nature as God has designed it and *is* in line with the words you read in the Bible as God has inspired it.

My hope for you is that you will keep searching for as much insight and wisdom as you can on this subject until you get God's answers for yourself, even if it takes years.

BUCKETS OF TEARS

I also fully realize that while telling people my story can produce great hope in some, it can also produce great anguish in others, depending on where they're coming from or where they're wanting to go.

To those who find it hopeful, I am thankful, and I pray it does encourage them as they continue on this journey. To those who find it hurtful, I'm so sorry.

Believe me when I say I could fill buckets with the tears I've cried for those who are facing these struggles; tears for those who have felt the weight of wondering why they have the attractions they have and why those attractions haven't changed in the ways they had hoped; and tears for those who have wrestled through this issue for years, but have not yet seen their breakthroughs come in the ways they've wanted them to come.

But I can also say I could fill buckets with the tears I've cried, tears of rejoicing, as I've watched people walk down the aisle with a man or woman of their dreams of the opposite sex because God has brought them so much healing and restoration in this area of their lives; tears of rejoicing with friends as they experience the birth and growth of children born to them who would have never been born had they stayed on the path which they were on; and tears of rejoicing with people who have found Christ and found a community within their church, sometimes for the first time in their lives, which is meeting some of their deepest needs for significance and connection, even if they have not yet met, nor may ever meet, one particular person to marry.

I say all of this to say that I'm not writing to you from a place of naiveté about the very real struggles that people face in this area. I'm also not writing from a place of judgment or condemnation, that if people just had more faith or more wisdom or better looks or different feelings, that things would turn out differently for them.

I'm writing from a place of having seen God do the miraculous in people's lives, in person after person after person, sometimes in ways which are as different and unique as the individuals themselves, but in ways which, when God has been invited in, have astounded and amazed all of us who have seen those miracles take place.

GREAT HOPE

There's a reason why talking about homosexuality feels like walking on eggshells. That's because it *is* like walking on eggshells. But the walk is worth it because people are worth it. We just need to do our best to walk with sensitivity.

As a writer named J. Masai has said about people in general: "Feelings are everywhere—be gentle." Regarding the topic of homosexuality, this is true even more. Homosexuality is a sensitive topic, affecting people in some of the deepest places of their beings. But just because it's a sensitive topic, that doesn't mean we can't take a sensitive approach to talking about it.

For me, the best approach to take in talking about this subject is one that was suggested by the Apostle Paul in a letter he wrote to the Christians living in Ephesus. I love the way it reads in *The Message* version of the Bible: "God wants us to grow up, to know the whole truth and tell it in love—like Christ in everything" (Ephesians 4:15, MSG).

God *does* want us to grow up, to be mature, and to know the whole truth. Then He wants us to tell the whole truth in love, like Christ in everything.

I'm guessing this is exactly what *you're* wanting in regards to this subject as well: to be mature, to know the whole truth, and to tell it in love, like Christ in everything.

While it may feel like walking on eggshells when talking to others about this subject, the truth is that God can use your words, your heart, and your actions to bring life to those around you. It may take time for people to change, but don't think that people aren't listening. Don't think that they're not hearing what you're saying. Sometimes they just need to think through what you're saying so they can come to their conclusions on their own.

People *are* listening. They *do* care what you think. And whatever you do, whatever you say, if you're seeking the whole truth, and telling it in love—like Christ in everything—then you can *absolutely* see miracles take place in people's lives for good and forever, both here on earth and in eternity.

Know that there is GREAT HOPE. What you have to offer to others is something they desperately need: your love, your care, your words, your touch, your kindness, your tears, your understanding; in sum, God's truth, wrapped up in love.

Study Guides for Chapters 1 & 2

After every two chapters in this book, I'd like to pause and give you a chance to reflect upon or discuss with others what you've just read.

If you're going through this book on your own, you might want to take out a pen or a mark-up tool to jot down your thoughts. If you're going through this book with a group, you can use these study guides to discuss the chapters as you go along.

One of the reasons I'm including these additional thoughts for reflection and discussion is because I've read that Jesus did something similar with those closest to Him.

Jesus loved telling stories. In fact, the Bible says, "He was never without a story when He spoke" (Mark 4:33b, MSG). But Jesus also loved expanding on those stories with those closest to Him, as the same passage says, "When He was alone with His disciples, He went over everything, sorting out the tangles, untying the knots" (Mark 4:34, MSG).

My hope with these study guides is to do for you what Jesus did with those closest to Him, going over everything, sorting out the tangles, and untying the knots, as it were.

To that end, each study guide includes a *Chapter Summary* and several *Questions For Reflection & Discussion*. I've included a study guide for *every* chapter, but have interspersed them after every *two* chapters in the book to make it easier for those who want to complete this study in six weeks, with an optional seventh week if you'd like to discuss the Conclusion and Afterword separately.

For group discussions, feel free to choose only a few questions from each chapter to discuss each week to allow ample time for people to talk. To help you decide which questions to discuss, I would suggest first using the questions which include Scripture references.

Please note that these study guides may be *the most important part of the whole book*, as this is where God might speak to you most clearly about each subject that is addressed.

Whatever way you do it, I pray that God speaks through it!

THE AUDIENCE FOR THIS BOOK

I'd also like to say a few words about the *audience* for whom I've written this book.

The same passage in the Bible which tells us that Jesus told stories and expanded on those stories also tells us that Jesus took into account His particular *audience* whenever He spoke. The Bible says: "With many stories like these, He presented His message to them, fitting the stories to their experience and maturity" (Mark 4:33a, MSG).

In the same way, I've written this book with a particular audience in mind.

Since the 2015 Supreme Court ruling which legalized gay marriage in all 50 states, the landscape has forever changed for gays here in the U.S. And like the shot heard round the world, that singular decision has also changed the landscape for gays worldwide.

While this ruling provides an option for gays who *want* to pursue their same-sex attractions to the fullest extent possible, it does little to help those who *don't* want to pursue their same-sex attractions, for whatever reason they may not want to pursue them. It's for this latter group that I've written this book, not just as readers, but also for those who love them.

If you know gays who are happy in pursuing their same-sex attractions to the fullest, then this book may not be for them. I know what it's like, and maybe you do, too, to have someone try to convince me of something that I've already looked into deeply, weighed all the facts as fully as I can, and come to a conclusion. To have someone try to convince me otherwise sometimes just sounds like a "noisy gong or a clanging cymbal" (1 Corinthians 13:1b, ESV).

My desire with this book is not to add any more hurt or pain to those who have often already endured enough hurt and pain for one lifetime.

I've written this book primarily for those who are *wrestling* with their same-sex attractions and for those who love them. I've written it for those who are wondering if there might be some alternative—any alternative—to dealing with their feelings of same-sex attraction which does *not* involve pursuing those attractions to their fullest.

I know many people who feel *trapped* in their attractions, as if they are locked into only one option for life. No one likes to feel caged like that. If you know someone who feels "stuck" in something in which they don't want to be stuck, trapped by feelings they've never asked for and never would have chosen on their own, even if they felt like they had a choice, then this book is for you.

This book is for those who want to pursue a different path with their life and for those who love them. I've written this book not merely as an academic exercise, but as a way to share with you a path I've taken myself and found to be extremely fulfilling—even more fantastic than I could have ever imagined. It's a journey which I can recommend wholeheartedly to anyone who wants to pursue it.

For those who are *not interested* in this option, but who are *still interested* in learning as much as they can about a topic that is near and dear to them, I believe this book will *still* be of great benefit, not only to them but also to those who love them—if for no other reason than to gain a better understanding of themselves and one another. I've written this book in a way that even those who have never had a same-sex attraction in their lives can understand and relate to those who have.

In the end, the *real beneficiaries* of this book will be those who will be *loved better* as a result of someone they know having taken the time to read it.

TWO *OTHER* BOOKS

Lastly, for readers who have not yet put their faith in Christ, or for Christians who would like to read a more *romantic* telling of my story (because it *is* a love story!), you might like to read my true story in novel form called *Fifty Shades of Grace*, which, for reasons of modesty, I've written under my pen name, Nicholas Deere.

Readers have called *Fifty Shades of Grace* "a gripping story," "a page turner, for sure" and "a story that all of us can relate to." As its title implies, the book contains a rather *sensual* telling of my story and, while tastefully told, some readers have found it to be surprisingly intimate. (Consider yourself warned!)

For readers who would like to read my story in the context of the "bigger picture" of what God has to say about sex *beyond* the topic of homosexuality, you might like to read my book, *What God Says About Sex.* This popular and practical little book has been helpful to readers of all ages who want to learn more about sex from a biblical perspective, including younger readers who are just learning about sex for the very first time.

With that introduction behind us, and for those wanting to keep reading *this* book (and I hope you will!), let's press on with the study guides for Chapters 1 and 2!

Eric Elder

STUDY GUIDE FOR CHAPTER 1: "MY TESTIMONY IN A NUTSHELL"

CHAPTER SUMMARY

The author's brief testimony conveys at least three things:
- that he went into homosexuality,
- that he came out of homosexuality through the power of Christ and with the help of a friend who later became his wife,
- and that he feels he's been living an abundant life ever since, for more than 30 years.

The author says he will also offer ideas throughout this book to help readers walk alongside those they love in what may be the most important journey of their lives.

QUESTIONS FOR REFLECTION & DISCUSSION

Read John 10:10. How do you think these words of Jesus could apply to the author's testimony?

Read John 20:30-31. In light of these verses, what are some reasons why people share their stories about what Jesus has done for them? What are some reasons why the author of this book might want to share his?

Read John 21:25. If Jesus touched so many people's lives when He walked the earth that the whole world couldn't contain them, and He's been alive and actively touching people's lives ever since, how might that thought encourage you regarding His ability to touch your life and the lives of those you love?

What thoughts came to mind when you first read the author's brief testimony? Did his story raise any questions? What *more* would you like to know about his story?

Have you ever heard a testimony similar to the author's, of a person who has experienced same-sex attractions, yet has gone on to live a long-term, deeply-fulfilling heterosexual life? If such a life were possible for you or for someone you love, would you want it for yourself or for that person? Why or why not?

Is there someone you know who might benefit from going through this book and this study with you? If so, would you consider asking them?

Has Jesus ever touched your life in a way that is similar to the way He touched the author's life, even if the details were different? If so, would you be willing to share your own "testimony in a nutshell" with those around you?

STUDY GUIDE FOR CHAPTER 2: "MY TESTIMONY IN AN EGGSHELL"

CHAPTER SUMMARY

Talking about homosexuality can sometimes feel like walking on eggshells. But just because this is a sensitive topic doesn't mean we can't talk about it in a sensitive way. Why? Because:

- *people want* to talk about it,
- *people have more questions* about it than ever before,
- and *people's lives can be changed* for good and forever, just like the author's life was changed when he read what someone else had to say about this topic.

The author says he's been afraid to share his testimony for two reasons over the years:

- for fear of what people who *hate* gays might think,
- and for fear of what people who *love* gays might think!

Yet the author continues sharing his testimony in hopes of helping those who are experiencing same-sex attractions but *don't* want to pursue them—for whatever reason they don't want to pursue them.

The author knows that some people may not accept what he has to say no matter what, yet he encourages readers to keep reading, saying like the blind man whom Jesus healed: "One thing I do know. I was blind, but now I see!"

QUESTIONS FOR REFLECTION & DISCUSSION

Read John 9:1-41. After being asked several questions about his healing, how did the blind man sum up what had happened to him (verse 25)? Why is this such a significant statement? How does the author relate this story to his own?

Do you find the topic of homosexuality coming up more and more in conversations these days? Why does the author think this can be a good thing? When this topic does come up, do you feel comfortable talking about it—or does it feel more like walking on eggshells?

Read Psalm 119:32. What does the psalmist say is the reason his heart has been set free? In what areas of our lives can this same reason also set *our* hearts free?

Read Ephesians 4:15. According to this verse, what does God want us to do and become? How will doing these things help us to grow into the likeness of Christ? Where do you see yourself on the "life cycle of learning" in regards to this topic?

Why will some people always remain unconvinced that real change is possible, at least according to the quote by David Swift and to the story of the man who thought he was dead?

In what ways might you apply J. Masai's quote, "Feelings are everywhere—be gentle," to your conversations regarding this or any other topic?

Chapter 3:
A Few Words About Attractions

———— ❖ ————

In which I share about the complexity of
attractions, where they come from, what to do
with them, and the fact that they can and do
change—sometimes quite significantly.

———— ❖ ————

In this book, you'll find that I often talk about "attractions." There's much debate about where attractions come from, whether they're inborn or not, whether they're shaped by circumstances or not, whether they're chosen or not, and whether they're changeable or not. Thankfully, I'm here to answer all your questions, definitively (he says, wryly).

The number one question I'm asked about homosexuality is this: "Do you think people are born gay?"

It's a valid question, and in this chapter, I'll give you a valid answer. But I think the more interesting question is this: "Why are people attracted to *anyone* they're attracted to?"

This story isn't in the Bible, but I've heard that Adam was talking to God one day about Eve.

Adam said, "God, why did you make her so beautiful?"

God said, "I made her that way, Adam, so that you would be attracted to her."

Adam thought for a moment, then said, "But, God, why did you make her so dumb?"

To which God replied, "I made her that way, Adam, so that she would be attracted to you."

(It's a joke which offends everyone equally, which my kids tell me is what makes it so funny.)

While *that* story about attractions isn't in the Bible, there are plenty of others which are, stories such as Jacob's attraction to Rachel (Genesis 28-30), David's attraction to Bathsheba (2 Samuel 11-12) or Amnon's attraction to Tamar (2 Samuel 13).

Each of these stories describes heartfelt attractions, yet all of them have dramatically different endings. Why? Because of the choices the people made about what to do with the attractions they were feeling—choices which either fulfilled or destroyed God's plans for their lives.

I've talked to hundreds of people in one-on-one conversations over the course of 30 years, and I'm always amazed at the responses I get when talking about people's attractions. People have wildly different attractions for wildly different reasons.

Some people like men with beards; others like men without. Some people like women with extensive curves; others like women with daintier forms. Some people think one actor is hot; others think the same actor is not. The reasons why people are attracted to other people vary about as much as the people themselves.

CHANGING ATTRACTIONS

An elderly friend once told me, after first meeting a man whom we both knew, that she thought he was one of the ugliest men she had ever met. Although he wasn't repulsive by any means, some of the features of his face were out of proportion to what she was used to seeing.

She went on to tell me, however, that after several months of getting to know him, she began to see him in a totally different way. He was a truly winsome man, and he won her over. Within a few months of thinking he was one of the ugliest men she had ever met, she came to see him as one of the most attractive men she had ever met.

I see this happen all the time, whether it's with boyfriends, girlfriends, spouses, or lovers, where a person who has had no particular attraction to someone else, somehow, suddenly finds that other person to be the sole object of their affections. I've seen people fall madly in love with other people who have previously not sparked even a flicker of interest in their hearts.

I've also seen this happen in reverse, where someone who was at one time wildly attracted to someone else, later—either suddenly or over a period of time—no longer had any attraction to that person whatsoever. The flame that had once burned so brightly had gone out completely. The person had "lost that lovin' feelin'," with not even a wisp of smoke left from the fire that once raged so strongly within.

What causes people's attractions to change so dramatically like this?

Oftentimes, *nothing* has changed in terms of the appearance or persona of the one being adored or abhorred, but *everything* has changed within the mind of the person doing the adoring or abhorring.

It's been said that the single most important sex organ in the body is the *mind*. After more than 30 years of hearing people's stories about what attracts them and what doesn't, I'm convinced that this is true.

I've also found something particularly insightful when talking to people with same-sex attractions, that is, attractions toward people who are the same sex as they are. People with same-sex attractions are not usually attracted to *everyone* of their own sex, but only to a small subset.

In talking with a man who has wrestled with same-sex attractions for many years, I asked if he was attracted to *all* men or only to *some*. He replied, "Only to some, and not to many at that."

While he was struggling with his attractions to *certain* men, he realized during our conversation that he wasn't attracted to *all* men, but, in fact, to only a *few*.

When I asked what *types* of men he was attracted to, he listed specific qualities and characteristics which he equated with what he longed for in a close friendship with a man. Even if he *was* born with an attraction to men, he certainly wasn't born with an attraction to *all* men, because he simply didn't *have* an attraction to all men, but only to a small subset of men.

BORN GAY?

Let me underscore this point even more. I was talking with an African-American man one day about his attractions toward men. When we started our conversation, he told me he was absolutely convinced he was born gay. Why else, he wondered, would he have had these feelings all his life?

When I asked him if he was attracted to all men, or only to some, he answered, "Only to some, for sure!"

This man then went on to tell me that there were men of a certain age above his and below his to which he was definitely *not* attracted. He also told me there were some types of men by which he was absolutely repulsed, because of the way they walked or talked or carried themselves, and with such men he would never consider a romantic relationship, no matter what.

Most telling of all, however, to both him and to me, was when he said that within that smaller subset of men, he was only attracted to white men. He had never, ever, not once, had an attraction to or an encounter with another African-American man.

After a few moments of taking in what he had just said, I asked, as gently as I could, "So what you're telling me is that when God created you, He created you both gay AND racist?"

The man burst out with a laugh at the irony of the truth that had just dawned upon him.

Although he may not have known the why's and wherefore's behind the attractions he had, he realized it was wrong to attribute his attractions to God or to nature just because he didn't know from where else they may have come.

In that moment, both this man and I could see that there was something about his attractions that were *not* due to the way he was wired from birth, but more likely from something else that was at play.

While there may have been something about the way he was designed from conception which played into the attractions he had, the fact that he was not attracted to all men, nor even to most men, but only to a particular subset of men with a particular subset of traits, made us both realize that there was probably more going on in his attractions than simply being "born gay."

Do I think there are reasons why we're attracted to certain people, some of which may have to do with the way God has wired us? Yes! Sometimes our reactions and responses to other people, and their reactions and responses to us, are indeed generated by particular features or traits that were given to us by God at birth. (And before this chapter ends, I'll share with you some of the reasons why *my* particular wiring made *me* particularly receptive to the advances of other men.)

But I also believe that there are reasons which go beyond our initial wiring at birth that cause us to be drawn to or repelled by certain people, regardless of their gender.

FEELINGS

When talking about homosexuality, we're talking about feelings. And feelings can change, sometimes within a moment of someone discovering that the person they love has been unfaithful or has been caught in a blatant lie or has formed a destructive habit. Conversely, feelings can change within a moment of someone having poured a glass of wine or gazing at a full moon or spreading out a blanket on a beach.

Feelings can also take longer to change, following the normal ebb and flow of a relationship as it either grows or fizzles.

As much as feelings change, however, it's also important to note that feelings can be incredibly *difficult* to change, oftentimes persisting long after someone might want them to persist.

I know what it's like to fall in love with someone who hasn't fallen in love with me, and no matter how hard I've tried to wish away or pray away those feelings, I've not been able to—certainly, that is, not in my own strength. Yet just because those feelings persist, it doesn't mean that God has ordained for me to *be* with that person (much to their relief, I can imagine!).

There are also people to whom I have been instantly attracted, but after one or two conversations with them, I have lost all attraction entirely.

Simple experience, both my own and what I've heard during hundreds of personal conversations, tells me that our attractions are complex, sometimes changeable, sometimes not, sometimes persistent no matter what we try, and sometimes cannot be resurrected, it seems, no matter what we try, either.

So in order to answer the question I promised you I would answer at the beginning of this chapter, when people ask me, "Do you think people are born gay?" it's important for me to know the question *behind* their question.

If what the person is asking me is this: "Are the feelings I have now, or the feelings I've had all my life, the same feelings I'm going to have tomorrow, or for the rest of my life," then my answer is "No, your feelings can and do change, and they can and could change in this area of your life as well."

But if what the person is asking me is this: "Is there something about the way God created me that has had an influence on the attractions I am feeling now, or have felt in the past?" then my answer is "Yes, the way God created you, and the way that you, and others, react and respond to the way God created you, could have some bearing on the attractions you're feeling now, and on the attractions you might feel in the future."

I'm not a psychologist, but I do know that people treat others differently based on the way God made them, whether they're black or white, tall or short, left-handed or right-handed, thin or curvaceous. And I know that the way people react to the way God created people certainly plays into their attractions or lack of attractions.

So, yes, I do believe that the way we are created does have a bearing on the attractions we feel and the attractions which others feel toward us.

But when people ask, "Do you think people are born gay?" they're often asking with vastly different motives. If they're people who have same-sex attractions and *want* to pursue those attractions, then they're often hoping the answer is, "Yes," so they can pursue their attractions without hindrance—at least not *that* hindrance. But if they're people who have same-sex attractions and *don't* want to pursue those attractions, people who feel trapped and hopeless in their situations, then they're often hoping the answer is, "No," giving them hope that change really is possible.

REPHRASING QUESTIONS

This is why I like to rephrase people's questions, not as a way to dodge their questions, but as a way to address the questions that are really on their hearts, which, in the case of the question of whether or not people are born gay is often simply this: "Do you think people's attractions can and do change?"

And to that question, my answer is a clear and resounding, "Yes! I do think people's attractions can and do change."

Then I go on to share with them some of the examples I've just shared with you.

For people who are feeling trapped and hopeless in their situation, this often gives them real hope, sometimes for the first time in their lives. For people who are looking for a reason to "go for" whatever they want to "go for," then it causes them to at least pause for a while, requiring them to think through a little more carefully what they're wanting and why they're wanting it.

The practical reality is that we can't simply "go for" anyone and everyone to whom we're attracted, whenever we find them attractive.

I've been attracted to several Hollywood stars, but I can't go for them. They often belong to someone else, and they might never be attracted to me.

I've also been attracted to people who are married and people who are already in committed relationships. I can't go for them, either, just because I'm attracted to them, or I would destroy the relationships they already have with others.

Even if a person who does have same-sex attractions eventually marries a person of their same sex, they would be deceiving themselves if they thought that by marrying that *one* person it would somehow eliminate *all of their other attractions* to anyone other than the person they've married.

Getting married doesn't suddenly eliminate people's attractions to others, not in gay marriages nor in straight marriages. What, then, will people who are married do with their unwanted sexual attractions toward others? Indulge those attractions? Or (heaven forbid!) deny them?

Hopefully, they'll choose the latter—for their sake, for God's sake, and for the sake of everyone involved.

We simply *can't* conclude that just because we feel sexually or romantically attracted to a person that God wants for us to "go for" that person. This is why God has laid out restraints for us, restraints which are written not only in the Bible but also in our hearts, such as "Thou shalt not commit adultery." God has laid out these restraints to protect us, to protect others, and to help us to attain the fullness of what He has in mind for our lives, including our love lives.

Are people born gay? While it's possible, it seems about as likely as saying that people are born racist. I'm not denying that the way we are created by God can and does influence the way that we react and respond to one another. But to attribute those feelings of attraction solely to God, or solely to nature itself, denies what to me is an obvious reality that there are certainly other forces at play as well.

INCITING INCIDENTS

In all of my conversations with men and women over the years, while I've found that a few of them *haven't* been able to identify any particular reasons as to why they might have attractions to those of their own sex, or why they might have aversions to those of the opposite sex, many of them *have* been able to pinpoint—with absolute clarity—the exact day, moment, incident, or reason which caused them to turn their attentions either toward or away from those of one sex or the other.

I've had women shared with me incidents that have led them to fear having intimacy with men. As such, they simply feel more comfortable with women.

It seems to follow, logically, at least, that if a particular event or circumstance caused someone's feelings of attraction to go in one direction, then, perhaps, another particular event or circumstance could cause that person's feelings of attraction to go in another direction.

This isn't to say it would be easy to change directions. But it is to say that, at least conceivably, such a change could be possible. And, with my own eyes, I have seen such dramatic reversals take place many times.

I've also had men tell me that because of the negative influence of one or a few domineering women in their lives—be it a mother, a sister or a previous lover—they now have no attraction whatsoever to *any* women. They feel constrained and constricted by such women and find they would simply rather be with men.

It seems to follow, then, that if their attractions were negatively affected by a few people's negative influences over them, then their attractions could also be positively affected by a few people's positive influences in the future.

Again, I'm not saying this is necessarily easy, and I've walked through this exact scenario with enough people over enough time to know just how difficult it can be, but I am saying it is conceivable, and *more* than conceivable, as, again, I have seen with my own eyes such changes take place.

All of this, of course, gets into the heady field of psychology, which abounds with a wide range of possibilities and opinions regarding people's attractions.

I wouldn't, however, even be suggesting these ideas had I not seen people actually discover the source of their attractions, work through the why's and wherefore's, and then move on to a different way of thinking and living which has brought them much more fullness, much more joy, and much more peace than ever before. (It also raises the age-old question: "How many psychologists does it take to change a lightbulb?" The answer: "Only one, but the lightbulb has to really want to change.")

MY JOURNEY INTO HOMOSEXUALITY

Let me bring this closer to home. I also said earlier in the chapter that I would share with you more about my own attractions and some of the factors I've pinpointed which caused me to be very receptive to going into homosexuality in the first place.

There is a sense in which I do believe that the way God has wired me has affected my attractions, and that is this: God has wired me with a very sensitive nature. I'm sensitive to people, I'm sensitive to pain, and I'm sensitive to subtleties in feelings and colors and textures in beauty and music and art.

I fully believe that God has wired me this way, and that He has wired me this way to accomplish His unique purposes in and through my life, just as He has wired others in other ways to accomplish His unique purposes in and through their lives.

This doesn't mean, however, that God has wired me for sex with other men.

A simple glance at the body parts involved quickly reveals that all of us, as humans, are wired for heterosexual sex. The parts simply fit together better that way, and they are designed to fit together in very specific ways for very specific reasons, including both intimacy and reproduction.

Beyond this "simple look" at the body parts involved, a more detailed study, whether in medical books or in light of practical experience, reveals the incredible intricacy with which the human reproductive system works. It is truly remarkable the way the parts fit together, from the way that stimulating the sexual organs makes sex possible at all to the way that the sperm and egg are united in order to spark life, enable a baby to grow, and eventually be delivered. (The human reproductive system is, to me, one of the most compelling natural evidences of God's existence.)

I've been at the birth of all six of my kids, and the way children are born is amazing. But I've also been at the conception of all six of my kids, and the way children are conceived is even more amazing!

From a sheer physical standpoint, it's fairly convincing to me that God has wired me, as a human being, for heterosexuality. *That's* the way I was born. To say otherwise would be to deny the "facts of life" as they are presented to me.

I don't believe that because I'm sensitive means that I was created by God to have sex with men. But what being sensitive has meant is that I've often been more inclined to art and music and drama and dance than to contact sports or rough-and-tumble play.

As such, growing up in the small town in which I did, I was often surrounded by women, many of whom shared some of these same characteristics and easily became some of my best friends.

I liked athletics, but not contact sports, so I took dance and gymnastics at a dance studio in a larger town nearby. Those classes often had 20 or 30 girls in each of them and, at most, only one or two other guys.

I liked music, and, after hearing a man from Switzerland play a flute when I was a child, which he said he played while hiking through the Swiss Alps, I thought it would be cool to play the flute someday, too. So when I had a chance to pick out an instrument to play in the school band, I picked out the flute. Over the years, I've often played in marching bands surrounded by women, rather than busting heads on the football field with other men.

I sang in the choir and acted in plays, which, once again, in the small town where I grew up, were activities dominated by women.

None of these activities, in and of themselves, made me gay. None of these activities made me want to have sex with a man. In fact, I was always amazed that some of the guys at school would call me gay because I did these things, yet I had more close friendships with women than any of the men I knew!

RELATING TO MEN

For me, as well as for many men who go into homosexuality, my problem *wasn't* in relating to women. Women were often among my best friends. My problem was in relating to men. I wasn't part of their culture. I wasn't part of their locker room banter. I wasn't part of their social clubs or drinking clubs or sports clubs.

I found it ironic that men who called me gay would then jump on top of each other on the football field to celebrate their victories or pat each other on their rear ends after a game, whether they were doing so in public on the field or in the shower room after a game in private.

The most macho men I knew rarely hung out with girls, certainly not as just friends, but rather hung out with other guys. ALL. THE. TIME. They called me gay, but they seemed to have closer physical and personal relationships with other men than I ever did.

I didn't have gay feelings at that time, but that didn't keep some of them from calling me gay, not based on my sexuality, but based on the activities in which I was involved. That made me feel out of sync with other guys.

And I did like girls! I had a few girlfriends in grade school and one significant relationship in high school. We were romantic, emotionally and physically, often holding hands, kissing, and taking long walks in the woods.

I loved the physical and emotional intimacy of these relationships. But we never had any sexual activity, as that wasn't something that seemed right to do until marriage.

When I went away to college, I met some guys who were truly interested in being my friend. Instead of making fun of my artistic talents, these men applauded those talents! They thought it was cool that I enjoyed singing and dancing and acting.

I couldn't believe there were guys who really understood me, appreciated me, and enjoyed being with me for who I was, not expecting me to be someone who I wasn't.

When one of these same guys later approached me to see if I'd be interested in *more* in our friendship, it didn't take me long to say "Yes." Even though having an intimate relationship with a man was foreign territory for me, and even though I had some initial reservations about the idea, it was still fairly easy for me to fall into it.

In fact, I loved it. I loved the attention, I loved that someone was attracted to me, and I loved the physical feelings that it produced.

Emotionally, having another man in my life in this way met a need deep within me for male friendship which I felt I had missed out on for so long, with physical affection thrown in as a bonus. For me, it was truly a case of "friends with benefits," as some people call such relationships.

Once I realized that sex seemed to be a pathway toward meeting this deep need for male friendship in my life, I found that my attractions to men were growing.

Like many women have done, I began seeking out men with whom I could be intimate so I could feel close to them as friends as well. And like many women, I soon discovered that when, at times, I did say "No" to sex, the friendship I thought I was gaining would end. After a few friendships ended like this, I realized that perhaps this wasn't the best way to go about making friends with men after all.

While my attractions to men were growing with every relationship, I wasn't quite sure this was the direction I wanted my attractions to grow.

But then I began to wonder if I had a choice. Although I wasn't gay in high school when my friends called me gay, I couldn't deny that I was now. I mean, the first person with whom I had ever been sexually intimate was a man, and I had only been sexually intimate with men ever since, so I guess that made me gay, right? Or did it?

And if I were gay, was this the way I was going to be forever? I wasn't quite sure what I thought about that idea.

Was I really *born* gay?

Chapter 4:

A Few Words About Being Gay

❖

In which I share what it means to be gay, why more people than you might think could be defined as gay, and why I never thought of myself as gay—even when I was.

❖

I never thought of myself as gay. In fact, I didn't even know what the word meant until some guys in school called me gay. I had to look it up at home in our family's *Webster's Collegiate Dictionary.* (It would be another 20 years until Google was born.)

The words of choice at that time varied between *gay, fag, sissy, queer,* and the especially derogatory *homo* (as in "You homo!" when walking down the hall to a class, or more typically, when walking through a crowded locker room after P.E., trying to squeeze your way through 25 other guys with whom you had just shared an open shower).

Sometimes the words were said in jest. Other times they were said in a spirit of true meanness.

When I looked up the word *gay,* it led me to the word *homosexual,* which was defined as "a person who is sexually attracted to members of one's own sex."

In today's terminology, the word *gay* is often defined similarly as "someone who is experiencing same-sex attractions." By using the term "same-sex attractions," the definition broadens the meaning a bit to include not only those who are *sexually* attracted to members of their own sex, but also to those who are *romantically* or *emotionally* attracted to members of their own sex, even if they are not necessarily *sexually* attracted to them.

In either of these definitions, I've found it interesting that homosexuality doesn't describe any particular *physical* characteristics of a person, but rather the *feelings* that a person is experiencing. As such, being gay isn't something that any scientist or any other person could identify in someone else with any degree of certainty without that person revealing it to them.

This isn't to say that there may not be some physical expressions of those feelings—because sometimes there are. But it would be like trying to ascertain if someone is hungry or not without that person telling you. You just can't tell if someone is hungry by simply looking at them, unless, of course, their hunger manifests itself in the way they act because of it.

By these definitions, *anyone* who has feelings of attraction toward anyone of their own sex could be considered gay. It doesn't take into account the degree to which they feel those attractions, whether strong or weak, or whether or not they have feelings toward someone of the opposite sex as well, to any degree.

It also doesn't take into account whether or not a person's feelings of attraction toward members of their own sex include *all* members of their own sex or just a *subset* of their own sex, however large or small that subset may be. If someone is experiencing, or has ever experienced, feelings of attraction toward someone of their own sex, sexually, romantically, or emotionally, then that person is, at least at the time of experiencing those attractions, gay.

This definition casts quite a broad net. And based on my conversations with people who have told me about their own feelings of attraction, this net includes many more people than you might ever imagine.

OBVIOUS OR OBLIVIOUS?

I've talked to people with same-sex attractions who are married with kids, who are single and celibate, who watch football on TV or ballet at the theater, and who look soft and effeminate or macho and tough.

Sometimes I have to hold myself back from speaking up when someone, say a wife or a mother, tells me that they can spot a gay a mile away, as if there's something about *every* person's outward expression that makes it *obvious* that they're gay, yet that same person can be *oblivious* to the fact that their own husband or child has just disclosed to me that they, too, have experienced same-sex attractions—they've just never shared those feelings with their wife or their mother because of what that person might think of them if they did.

So while it might be possible to spot *certain types* of gays, it's incredibly difficult to recognize the wide variety of people all around us, every day, who are experiencing same-sex attractions—many of whom you might never guess were gay.

Why? Because our *feelings* take place inside our hearts and our minds and are only expressed outwardly if we choose to express them (or if we happen to reveal them inadvertently).

What we see on the *outside* of a person does not always reveal what's going on *inside* of that person. As God told the prophet Samuel, when Samuel was looking for the next leader of Israel: "Do not consider his appearance or his height... Man looks at the outward appearance, but the Lord looks at the heart" (from 1 Samuel 16:7).

Why is this important to know? Because if we're going to talk about how to love *gays* better, it's important to know that *the definition of gays* includes people you may have never suspected had such attractions.

There may be nothing in the way they walk or talk or act, or nothing in what they do or don't do that would give you a clue.

Whenever I speak about this topic publicly, people come up to me afterwards, whether in public right there on the spot or in private at a later time, to reveal to me that they, too, have had same-sex attractions. The first words which often come out of their mouths are words like these: "I have never told anyone else about this in my life, but because of what you've shared, I feel like I can tell you."

One such man was married with kids. He came up to me after a talk to ask me how I dealt with the shame of it all, having same-sex attractions like he was having.

I asked him a little more, and he told me that he was in the navy. He said that when some of his shipmates would joke about homosexuality, he would join right in and joke back with them. But he confessed to me that he was secretly having sex with some of the other men on board. The shame of it all was killing him.

Had he not revealed his secret to me, I would have never suspected that he had feelings of attraction for other men, nor, I imagine, would his wife or his children or his shipmates, apparently, except for those with whom he had been intimate.

It's important to know that *anyone* you talk to may or may not be experiencing same-sex attractions—and what you say in those situations really matters.

I have a long-time friend who has struggled with same-sex attractions his entire life. Yet in all those years, he has hardly told anyone around him about his struggles. He told me recently that one of his best friends, a married man whose family has been a tremendous blessing to him, has a habit of regularly making derogatory comments about gays—comments which sting. My friend, while oftentimes *wanting* to voice his objections, says he's afraid to say anything for fear of jeopardizing their very dear and valuable friendship. The married friend simply doesn't understand the pain he is inflicting on one of his best friends.

Another man I know said he's in a men's group where the men will sometimes talk about their struggles with pornography. He said he was thankful that he didn't have that problem—at least he thought he didn't until one day when he stumbled upon some gay porn.

He found himself being drawn into what he was seeing and soon was himself addicted to porn—gay porn. This man was as surprised by what was happening to him as anyone else would have been. Unfortunately, he felt like he couldn't share his struggle with the other men in his group because of how they might react. He said he only shared it with me because of what I had shared in my testimony.

The reason I'm sharing this with you is because the guys in his men's group will never know that one of their group members, a man with whom they meet each and every week, struggles with gay porn. Unless this man chooses to reveal his secret to them, the men in his group might continue to think that same-sex attraction is a rare struggle. It's not. It's much more common than you might think, but few men like to talk about it.

ALL GAYS ARE NOT ALIKE!

Another common misconception is to think all gays are alike. Remember, for instance, my new friend from Chapter 2 who said the gays she knows are "loving, generous, and kind"? While some of the gays I know are indeed "loving, generous, and kind," I have met others who are "hateful, stingy, and snarky." Some are outright mean. And some use bullying tactics that would rival any of the straight bullies I ever encountered in school.

While there may be *some* common characteristics among *certain types* of gays, there simply isn't one set of characteristics which defines *everyone* who has ever had same-sex attractions.

This shouldn't be surprising, as there isn't one set of characteristics that defines everyone who is a teacher (my 3rd grade English teacher was radically different from my high school physics teacher) or everyone who is a professional athlete (imagine a tennis pro changing places for a day with a linebacker on a football team).

I've met women with same-sex attractions who are among the most beautiful women I've ever known (some have been professional models), while others I've met are among the roughest, toughest, and "manliest" women I've ever known (some would make good bouncers at a bar).

I've met men with same-sex attractions who are as chiseled as Michelangelo's statue of *David* (and who have made careers for themselves in front of television cameras), and others who look as attractive as a mug shot (some of whom have, in fact, been imprisoned for their sex crimes, regardless of their looks).

Then there's me. I think of myself as a fairly "ordinary" guy who grew up on a farm in the heart of the Great Midwest. I've lived most of my life as close to Normal as you can get. (There's a joke in there... I live about 20 miles from a city *called* Normal. When I moved to Plano, Texas for a year, a friend remarked, "How exciting for you, to move from Normal, Illinois to Plano, Texas." I mean, how much more "ordinary" can one guy get?)

I say all of this to emphasize that people with same-sex attractions come in all kinds of shapes and sizes.

As I mentally scan through all the people who have ever shared with me about their same-sex attractions, the vast majority of them are quite "ordinary," too. Maybe that's because my own "ordinariness" draws them out to speak to me when they hear my testimony, seeing in me someone with whom they could relate and share about their own feelings and struggles.

But whatever the reason, I meet with "ordinary" people all the time who are dealing with same-sex attractions, making it clear to me there are a *lot* of people dealing with these attractions, many of whom you would never guess.

You might not hear from all of us, however, just like you might have never heard from me before reading this book, because, frankly, it's something that is *really, really* hard to share with people.

Our feelings of attraction are so personal, so close to the heart, and they affect our interactions with so many people every day. Men especially already find it hard enough to talk about their innermost thoughts and feelings, not to mention their innermost thoughts and feelings regarding sex, not to mention their innermost thoughts and feelings regarding their same-sex attractions!

CELIBATE SIMPLETONS?

Some people think, mistakenly, that people in ministry like me might not be able to understand people in the "real world," people who struggle with "real problems."

But people in the ministry who are worth their salt hear more about the real trials and tribulations of those around them than most other professionals or lay people in the world.

A British pastor in the early 1900s, G. K. Chesterton, wrote a clever series of mystery books about a short, stumpy priest named Father Brown who had an "uncanny insight into human evil."

In one of Chesterton's stories, when a notorious criminal is caught by Father Brown—the same priest whom the criminal had previously called a "celibate simpleton"—the priest explains to the criminal, in precise detail, *how* he was able to detect and catch him in his crime.

The criminal then exclaimed: "How in blazes do you know all these horrors?"

To which the priest responded: "Oh, by being a celibate simpleton, I suppose. Has it never struck you that a man who does next to nothing but hear men's real sins is not likely to be wholly unaware of human evil?"

I wouldn't even be able to guess how many hours I've sat and listened to people tell me some of the most heartbreaking and tragic stories you could ever hear.

Why am I telling you this? To let you know that while people may not be telling *you* about their struggles in this area, they're definitely telling *me*—and I don't want you to be unaware of those things which the people around you may be wrestling with every day.

Bringing people's real-life struggles to light is one of the reasons I've written this book. I hope to heighten your awareness of what's going on inside those around you so that when you *do* speak about this issue, you can speak about it in a way that will *lift people up, not tear people down*—even if those people never reveal to you their own same-sex attractions.

If you've been unaware up to this point about how many people around you are experiencing same-sex attractions, don't feel bad. I've met some of the most sincere, compassionate, and kindhearted Christians who simply don't realize it, either.

I was recently preparing to give a talk to a group of about 300 youth at a church. When I ran into a woman at a coffee shop who went to that church, and I mentioned that I was preparing a talk on this topic, she said, "Oh, do you think some of the kids in that group are dealing with this?"

I almost choked on my breakfast sandwich when she said it. From the number of groups that I've addressed, even if it's 10 or 20 or 30 people, at least some portion of that group is either dealing with same-sex attractions themselves or they know of someone very close to them who is, let alone in a group of *300* youth whose hormones are raging as wildly as the questions that are running through their heads. They're wondering if their attractions mean they're gay. They're wondering what other people will think of them if their attractions are discovered. They're wondering if they should ask out a girl or a guy or just stay home and cry.

By bringing this reality to light, I'm in no way faulting anyone for not realizing that this issue affects more people than they might think. *That's why I'm sharing this with you!*

I want you to know, because if you don't know, you can't care, at least not in the way I believe you would want to care if you did know— which, I believe, is why you're reading this book at all.

SILENT CRIES

You might have noticed that some people wear their sexual preferences on their sleeves, whether to attract attention to themselves or to advertise their availability or just because they've stopped caring what other people think. Some are "out and loud" and sometimes draw the lion's share of the attention.

Yet many, *many* more people might never tell another soul about their same-sex attractions ever in their entire lives. That is, they won't tell anyone unless they feel that they've found someone whom they feel they can trust implicitly, who is *for* them, who cares about them enough to walk with them through their struggle. Even then, it still might take *years* until they're ever able to talk about it.

I have friends that I've known for more than a decade, friends with whom I've shared my testimony, friends with whom we've shared some of our most precious, innermost thoughts and feelings, who, only after all that time have finally confided in me that they've had similar feelings and attractions for others.

Whether it's because of their shame, their fear, or their uncertainty about what to do with their feelings, they've never felt they could tell anyone about their attractions, not even me, until they reached a tipping point where they needed help more than they needed to keep it a secret.

Even for me, having shared my testimony many times over the years in talks and books and articles, it's still hard for me to admit that I was gay. Being gay carries with it certain connotations with which I've never wanted to be associated.

Yet, based on what I've done and the attractions that I've felt, I have to admit that I was gay. And according to the dictionary definitions, where all it takes is experiencing a feeling of attraction toward someone of my same sex, I certainly was. I just don't like admitting it, even after all these years.

ON A SCALE FROM 0 TO 10

I also think it's important to share with you that the terms "gay" and "straight" are not as binary as you might think, (by binary, I mean either one or the other, exclusively).

One of the most significant observations I've made from my own conversations with those who are experiencing same-sex attractions is that their attractions not only vary in the *degree* to which they are attracted to one person or another, but also in the *mix* of attractions they feel toward members of both sexes.

I've found this to be true in so many cases, that when I'm helping people think through their sexual attractions, I will often ask them where they would put themselves on a scale of 0 to 10, with 0 meaning they are only attracted to people of their same sex, and 10 meaning they are only attracted to people of the opposite sex. Rarely has anyone with same-sex attractions ever told me they would put themselves at 0, meaning they have *never* had any attraction whatsoever to a person of the opposite sex.

And even in the rare cases where people *have* said they've been at a 0 on that scale, they told me they haven't been there forever.

I have a good friend who said he would have put himself at a 0 for the first *33 years* of his life. In all those 33 years, he had never, not once, not ever, had even one sexual attraction toward a woman.

Yet one day, while sitting out on a beach with a female friend, he suddenly went from a 0 to a 10! It was such a defining moment for him that it changed the course of the rest of his life!

My friend was absolutely stunned. He had never experienced such a thing, and he wasn't sure *what* to think about it! His whole mindset changed that day, and within a few short years, he was married to a woman who also moved his dial from 0 to 10 the instant they met. My friend and his wife have now been married for over twenty years and have had two children together along the way.

While this friend's story might be more extreme than what others have told me, in that he went for so many years without ever having an opposite-sex attraction, it points to the fact that people's attractions can and do change, even after very long periods of time, not only *within* the categories of gay or straight, but also *between* those two categories.

From my own experience, and from the experiences of those with whom I've talked, most people with same-sex attractions have a mix of attractions, rather than being exclusively at one end of the spectrum or the other. And, as I've mentioned earlier, even *those* attractions vary widely depending on the particular people to whom they find themselves attracted or not attracted.

While it's clear to me from hundreds of such conversations that sexual attractions are complex, wide-ranging, and on a continuum, I still find that many people think of sexual orientation as something that is rigid and fixed: that someone is either gay, straight, or bisexual. (And if you're going to include bisexuality in the list of categories, and you take into account that people have varying degrees of attraction *within* each of these categories, then you're really talking about *the whole range* of attractions from 0 to 10.)

PUZZLING CONVERSATIONS

This brings us back to the idea that sexual orientation is not quite so binary as people are led to believe, but occurs along a continuum instead. These conclusions have led to some very confusing conversations with people who insist on using the categories, well, *categorically*, meaning "unambiguously explicit and direct."

In one such conversation, I had an email from a man who had read my story about having had sexual relationships in the past with men.

He was very gracious, but in the middle of his note he wrote, "If you've had sex with a man, you're gay; just admit it."

I wrote back to him, as kindly as I could, saying, "But I've also had sex with a woman on a regular basis for well over 20 years, and I've never again had sex with another man, so I'm wondering what that makes me?"

To that he simply replied that I was still gay and just repressing it. Others have suggested that I was never gay in the first place, but just experimenting. Still others have said I must be bisexual, then, since I could happily go either way, which, by the way, seems to negate the argument that people *can't* somehow move from one end of the spectrum to the other.

Another person wrote to me saying she didn't believe anyone could ever go from being attracted to someone of their own sex to being attracted to someone of the opposite sex.

She said that although she had never had sex with anyone, she *knew* that she was a lesbian and would never be able to change.

After telling her my story in more detail, she concluded: "Well, if you love having sex with your wife now, then you must have never really been gay in the first place."

This was coming from a woman who had never in her life had a sexual encounter with another woman, yet she considered herself a lesbian, and unchangeably so. Yet, she also concluded that I, who *had* been intimately involved with several men for several years, was never *actually* gay, because I was now completely in love with a woman beyond my dreams.

Conversations like these are sometimes puzzling to me, and sometimes infuriating to those with whom I'm speaking, because the reality of what I'm presenting to them doesn't match the pseudo-reality they have created in their own minds. (And it makes me think, once again, of the man who believed he was dead, yet who said, after pricking his finger and watching it bleed, "What do you know? Dead men *do* bleed!")

The truth is that many people are *feeling* their way through this issue, not *thinking* their way through it.

How straight does one have to be to be considered straight, or how gay to be considered gay, or how near to the middle to be considered bisexual?

While these categories might be useful for generalizing people's feelings of attraction, they are not very useful for describing the reality that our feelings and attractions can and do move along a continuum, based on various factors at various times and in response to various people to various degrees.

Real change in our lives is not only possible, but is strongly encouraged throughout the Bible in verses like this one: "Do not conform any longer to the pattern of this world, but be transformed by the renewing of your mind. Then you will be able to test and approve what God's will is—His good, pleasing and perfect will" (Romans 12:2). And if the single most important sexual organ in the body is the mind, this verse can give great hope to those who are hoping for real transformation!

In my own case, and in the cases of many people I've had the pleasure of meeting in person, I've seen dramatic transformations take place in the hearts and minds of many people regarding this topic. I've seen people move from one end of the spectrum to the other, often in ways that have brought lasting joy and fulfillment beyond what *anyone* could have possibly imagined.

In the next chapter, I'll share how that change took place in my own life.

Study Guides For Chapters 3 & 4

STUDY GUIDE FOR CHAPTER 3: "A FEW WORDS ABOUT ATTRACTIONS"

CHAPTER SUMMARY

We all have strong attractions, yet we can't assume that God wants us to "go for" everyone to whom we're attracted:

- Jacob loved Rachel and it ended well (Genesis 28-30),
- David loved Bathsheba and people died (2 Samuel 11-12),
- and Amon loved Tamar and was killed (2 Samuel 13).

God wants us to direct our attractions toward the purposes for which He has given them to us.

Some people wonder if attractions can change or not. The author shares several stories of people who:

- have been in love, but then have "lost that lovin' feeling,"
- have been just friends, but then find "there's something there that wasn't there before,"
- and have been in gay relationships, but then have fallen in love with, and married, someone of the opposite sex.

People's attractions can and do change, sometimes quite significantly. We all have valid needs, but God wants us to meet those valid needs in valid ways.

QUESTIONS FOR REFLECTION & DISCUSSION

Read Genesis 29:17-20 (or the whole story in Chapters 28-30), 2 Samuel 11:2-4 (or the whole story in Chapters 11-12), and 2 Samuel 13:1-2 (or the whole story in Chapter 13). Why did each of these three stories which deal with strong attractions end so differently?

Why are some people strongly attracted to certain attributes or characteristics when other people aren't attracted to those same attributes or characteristics at all? What are some factors that might play into such attractions or lack of attractions?

Have you ever been strongly attracted to someone until getting to know them better, or conversely, not been strongly attracted to someone until getting to know them better?

What are some factors that can change people's attractions to others? Why do people sometimes "lose that lovin' feeling" and at other times find "there's something there that wasn't there before"?

Read Romans 2:14-15. What role do our consciences play in our decision making? How can people "know" what God wants them to do—even if they've never read the Bible?

Some people know exactly what caused their attractions to those of their same sex or their repulsion to those of the opposite sex. Are you aware of any particular incidents or events that may have influenced those attractions in yourself or someone you love? If that's the case, could another positive incident or event possibly cause those attractions to change once again in another direction?

What do you think about the statement: "It's been said that the single most important sex organ in the body is the *mind*."

Have you ever noticed that you or someone you know has been like the African-American man described in this chapter who was only attracted to very particular traits in a person? What roles do you think nature, nurture, and life experiences might play into such attractions?

Have you ever experienced attractions that were hard to contain, no matter how hard you've tried? Or, on the flip side, attractions that were hard to rekindle no matter what you've tried?

Why does the author believe he was drawn to relationships with those of the same sex? What do you think about the idea that men with same-sex attractions often don't have a problem in their relationships with women, but in their relationships with men?

If people think it's wrong to deny the strong attractions that they feel within them, what should such people do who get married and still have such attractions to people other than their spouse? What are some reasons why God might *want* us to deny our attractions, no matter how strongly we feel them?

STUDY GUIDE FOR CHAPTER 4: "A FEW WORDS ABOUT BEING GAY"

CHAPTER SUMMARY

The author shares three things about being gay:

- being gay involves *feelings* of attraction toward those of the same sex, whether those feelings are sexual, romantic, or emotional,
- and since feelings take place in the heart and mind, there's no way to identify someone as gay unless they expressly reveal it in their words or actions,
- as such, many more people can be wrestling with same-sex attractions without anyone else knowing.

This is why it's so important to take care with our words, because even people closest to us may be experiencing same-sex attractions and are listening to the words we say and the attitudes of our hearts.

The author states that most of the people with same-sex attractions with whom he has talked have had a *mixture* of attractions toward both men and women. He adds:

- while people often use the terms gay, straight, or bisexual, reality shows that people's feelings toward those of the same sex or the opposite sex would be better plotted on a continuum, rather than categorically at one end or the other or in the middle,
- very few of the hundreds of people to whom he has personally talked about their same-sex attractions have ever said they were only attracted to those of the same sex,
- and because of these factors, many more people could be identified as gay than people might realize.

Real change in *all* areas of our lives is not only possible, but is strongly encouraged throughout the Bible in verses like this: "Do not conform any longer to the pattern of this world, but be transformed by the renewing of your mind. Then you will be able to test and approve what God's will is—His good, pleasing and perfect will" (Romans 12:2).

The author says he has seen and experienced many such transformations like this, where people have moved from one end of the continuum to the other, often in ways that have brought lasting joy and fulfillment beyond what *anyone* could have possibly imagined.

QUESTIONS FOR REFLECTION & DISCUSSION

Read 1 Samuel 16:7. Why are matters of the heart so difficult to read in someone else? Since being gay is primarily about *feelings* of attraction rather than any physical characteristic, what's the only way you can tell if someone is experiencing same-sex attractions or not?

Read Romans 12:1-2. What do these verses say that it takes for us to be transformed? Given that some people say the mind is the most powerful sex organ in the body, what do these verses say about our ability to transform our sexual desires as well?

Are you surprised to hear that very few gays are attracted *solely* to those of their same sex, but rather have a *mixture* of attractions toward both sexes? Why or why not? How does this information change your view of whether or not gays can "change" from being attracted to one sex or the other?

If you are experiencing same-sex attractions, or know of someone who is, where would you place yourself, or the person you know, along the continuum of attractions from 0 to 10, with 0 being solely attracted to those of the same sex and 10 being solely attracted to those of the opposite sex? (No need to answer aloud!) How might this information be helpful to people as they think through this issue?

Given that same-sex attractions take place in the hearts and minds of those who are experiencing them, how likely is it that people around you might be experiencing such attractions without you even being aware of it? How might knowing this affect what you say or do around others?

Why might it be easier for people to open up about their same-sex attractions to some people rather than to others? If you truly wanted to help people in this area, what could you say or do to encourage others to share more freely with you about their attractions—without having to endorse homosexuality?

What might you say to someone who feels it would be impossible for their feelings of attraction to *ever* change toward those of the opposite sex, after having read the author's story and the other stories in this book—including the man who had never felt an attraction toward anyone of the opposite sex until he was 33?

Given what you've learned that most people who are experiencing same-sex attractions also have opposite-sex attractions to some degree, does that imply that a person must be gay if they've engaged in sex with someone of the same sex? And if that person has engaged in sex with someone of the opposite sex, does that imply that such a person must be straight? While the words gay, straight, and bisexual may be helpful as broad categories, why are these terms sometimes more complicating than helpful in discussions about this topic?

Chapter 5:

The Value Of A Loving Friend

———— ❖ ————

In which I share how I came out of
homosexuality, how my attractions changed
over time, and the value of a loving friend.

———— ❖ ————

If I were to plot my own attractions on a line from 0 to 10, with 0 being attracted only toward men and 10 being attracted only toward women, I would put myself, at various points in my life, somewhere in between those two endpoints. While the particular points have shifted at times from one side to the other, I have always had a mix of attractions.

I find that I'm attracted to *people*, regardless of gender. The danger for me and for all of us, regardless of where we find ourselves on that line, is when our attractions turn romantic or sexual.

We're all "attracted" to certain people, whether movie stars or next-door neighbors or co-workers or friends at church. Our attractions aren't the problem. The problem is when those attractions become romantic or sexual, something which God has reserved for us only within His well-defined boundaries.

In high school, I would plot my attractions at a point on the line somewhere around a strong 7 or 8. I was attracted to women. I liked being around them, I found them easy to talk to, and, as I mentioned before, women were often my best friends.

At the same time, however, I also found myself attracted to men, although to a much smaller degree. I found men to be mysterious and intriguing. I was drawn to those who were good looking or talented. And I occasionally had thoughts about men in ways that were sexual. Overall, I wished I could have been their friend.

But the idea of being in *a romantic or sexual relationship* with a man simply wasn't an option, neither in my mind nor in reality.

If I felt that sexual intimacy with a woman before marriage didn't seem like the right thing to do, as I mentioned in Chapter 3, then sexual intimacy with a man seemed even less so.

I also didn't know anyone who was gay at that time, or at least I didn't know people who admitted they were gay. I later learned that some of my friends in high school had, in fact, been involved in gay relationships during those years.

I certainly never talked about my feelings of attraction toward men. Although those feelings were there, they weren't significant. I felt like there was nothing I could have done with my feelings even if I had wanted to.

A SUDDEN SHIFT

When I moved away to college, and my girlfriend and I had gone our separate ways, I found myself still strongly attracted to women. I dated several and spent more than a few incredible nights of kissing on the quad, noting in my journals afterwards thoughts like this: "I could have kissed her all night!"

It wasn't until the summer between my freshman and sophomore years that my attractions began to shift. I had started making friends with some guys on campus who seemed genuinely interested in my life.

When some of those guys wanted to take our friendships further, whatever barriers I had before finally came down. I didn't resist.

My attractions and desires quickly swung to the other end of the scale. I would plot them at that time as being a strong 2 or 3.

Because those relationships with men were my first-ever sexual relationships, and because they met a valid need in my life for close male friends, I began to seek out more friendships like them. It was as if the gravitational pull on my desires had shifted, and my compass now pointed in the opposite direction.

I was still attracted to women, and I continued to enjoy some great female friendships. But because I was also finding some of my deepest needs being met by men for the first time, I found those relationships to be more and more enticing.

That's when I began to wonder if what my gay friends were telling me was really true: "Once gay, always gay, Eric." These friends seemed to have a point, and their own sexual journeys seemed to indicate that this had been their genuine experience.

Even if my gay friends were saying this to me with less than genuine motives in mind, whether to justify their own actions or to keep me in their circle of intimate friends a little while longer, I had to wonder if what they were saying about "once gay, always gay" was true.

Since I had never been sexually intimate with a woman, I wondered how I would know unless I tried sex with a woman, too. So I considered trying, just to see. I asked a friend whom I thought might be willing to try it with me, but thankfully, as I look back on it now, that door with my friend was closed.

After listening to various men over the years who have tried to have sex with a woman just to see if they liked it, rather than from a deep and genuine love for that woman, I've learned that such attempts often fall flat—for obvious reasons.

Sex is a wonderful *extension* of intimacy, but as a *substitute*, it will never compare.

Not sure what else to do, I kept doing what I was doing. I got involved with another man on campus and began thoroughly enjoying our close friendship.

Homosexuality was meeting a deep need in my life, and it had the further benefits of allowing me to have sex without the fear of someone getting pregnant, and, at least from my standpoint, not having to think about the relationship ever becoming a long-term one. That just wasn't on my radar.

Gay marriage wasn't a legal option anywhere in the whole world (and it wouldn't be legalized in *any* country for another 17 years), and having an *openly* gay relationship simply wasn't an option for me. I didn't see how I could ever endure the ridicule.

I never even thought about the fear of contracting a sexually transmitted disease. Believe it or not, AIDS had not yet been identified when I first went into homosexuality. It was three months *after* I began my first gay relationship that the term AIDS was coined to describe this "new" disease that was plaguing gay men almost exclusively at that time, or those who had come into contact with the blood of gay men.

All in all, homosexuality seemed to be, at least for me, a fairly risk-free, low commitment, and highly gratifying experience. I loved it. I truly did. While I didn't see homosexuality as a long-term option for my life, I was enjoying it enough that I didn't put too much more thought into pursuing an alternative.

That is, I didn't give it much more thought until I had a "beach encounter" of my own, like my friend's beach encounter which I mentioned earlier—only mine was with the woman who eventually became my wife.

MY JOURNEY OUT OF HOMOSEXUALITY

I had met Lana about a year earlier in a professional business fraternity on campus. She was cute and funny, and I even walked her home one night after spending a whole day hanging out with her on a field trip to another city with our professional business fraternity.

That night, I gave her a goodnight kiss at the door to her apartment. I wrote about that wonderful day and that kiss that night in my journal, adding these words at the end: "But I don't think much will come of it."

And it didn't. At least, not until about a year later, when I started talking to Lana about a road trip I was planning to take to the East Coast. I knew she loved to travel, so I asked her if she'd like to come along. She said she'd love to. I had asked her as just a friend, nothing more, since I was already dating this other man (unknown to her or to anyone else, really).

What I didn't know when I asked her to take that road trip was that the year before, on the night that I gave her that goodnight kiss at her door, she wrote a letter to her best friend saying that she had just met the man she was going to marry! Lana didn't tell *me* that, of course, not then, for sure, and not even until after we were married! She shared it with her friend and no one else, holding it close to her heart the whole time.

When we set out on that road trip to the East Coast, I wasn't thinking about a romantic or sexual relationship with her at all.

But one night, while walking along the beach and talking about love and romance in general (I had never talked to her about my same-sex attractions), we sat down on the beach and enjoyed a bottle of white wine together. Whether it was the moon and the stars or the wine and the waves or just her luscious-looking lips, I leaned over and kissed her. And she kissed me back.

Something happened in that moment that moved my dial instantly from a 2 or 3 to a 10! As the line says in a song from *Beauty and the Beast*, there was suddenly "something there that wasn't there before."

When people ask me if attractions can change, I have no hesitation in saying, "Yes!!! Absolutely!!!"

We started that trip as friends but came home as something much, much more. I had never experienced that kind of love, that kind of emotion, that kind of attraction to anyone in my whole life, male or female. It was off the charts.

When I got home from that trip, I faced a dilemma. I was still really enjoying my close friendship with this guy I was dating, but I was now also head-over-heels in love with Lana. Like others do when they're caught in such a dilemma and don't know what to do, I just kept dating both. When I was with my gay friend, I fully enjoyed our gay life. But when I was with Lana, I fully enjoyed our straight life.

As the weeks went on, I became more and more conflicted in my thoughts and feelings. I knew I couldn't continue going in two such opposite directions without it tearing me apart, and most likely them as well.

Aside from the dilemma of dating two people at once, which I felt was inherently wrong, I had the additional dilemma of wondering if I should keep "going for" the gay life or try "going for" the straight life. Both options offered something real and deep and satisfying, but I knew I couldn't have both forever.

I also knew that my dilemma went beyond deciding between the two personalities of the two people involved, but deciding about which path I was going to pursue in life.

I was torn, absolutely torn. I didn't feel like I had anyone I could talk to about it. My straight friends didn't know about my gay life, and my gay friends were assertively telling me, "once gay, always gay."

I wish I could describe the very real anguish I felt at having to make such a significant decision. At the same time, I'm glad I *can't* describe it to you, because it was, in a word, *unbearable.*

I didn't want to give up the meaningful friendships I was enjoying with my male friends after having waited so long to experience genuine companionship like that. But I also didn't want to continue in a direction which I could see wasn't going to take me to where I ultimately wanted to go.

When I looked deep into my future, I *really did* hope to have a wife and kids someday, and I hoped to be in a relationship that was open, not secretive, so I could tell others about the most incredible person in my life. (Looking back on that decision today, I realize that some of these factors which concerned me back then no longer exist, at least not to the same extent, but those were the reasons at the forefront of my mind at that time. Other reasons have kept me from wanting to go into homosexuality since that time, as I share in Chapters 9 and 11.)

I knew this was a decision that was going to impact the course of the rest of my life. At the core of my being, I could only see one path that would take me where I ultimately wanted to go.

MY DECISION

After weeks of wrestling with my conflicting thoughts, desires, and emotions, I made my decision. Now I was going to have to tell it to the two people I cared about most in the world.

I told my gay friend first, who took it hard, but who had seen it coming. He knew I had feelings for Lana ever since she and I took our trip to the East Coast.

He also knew I was wrestling with the concept of "once gay, always gay," and whether or not it was ultimately true. As difficult as it was for him, he didn't try holding me back from doing what he could tell was truly on my heart.

I knew this was a momentous decision, but even *I* didn't know at the time that when I said goodbye to him that night, I would be saying goodbye to the last gay relationship I would ever have.

The next day, I knew I was going to have to tell Lana about the decision I had made, which meant I was also going to have to confess to her my same-sex attractions—and the fact that I had been dating a man at the same time as I was dating her.

I knew it was going to be a heart-stopping conversation, and I had no idea how she might react. It was a gamble that she would even *want* to keep dating me after what I was about to tell her.

While I felt I had so much to lose by telling her, I couldn't imagine trying to build a future relationship with her without telling her this deep, dark secret in my life. It seemed only fair to her, and it seemed like it would have torn me apart if I had tried to keep it to myself.

I called Lana and asked if we could get together and talk about something that was on my heart. That night, with more than a few false starts and several lumps that kept catching in my throat, I told her for the first time about my attractions to men, my fears of what that might mean for my life, and the fact that I had been actively involved with a man even up to the day before.

LANA'S RESPONSE

Lana's response blew me away. She told me, in effect: "I love you, Eric. I always have. And I'll walk with you through this, too."

I never once, not that day nor any day thereafter, ever felt anything but love from Lana regarding my struggles with homosexuality. I never once felt condemned, looked down upon, nor anything other than supported and lifted up.

I don't know how she did it, and I don't know how to tell anyone else how to do what she did, either. All I know is that her response that night, and the way she responded whenever the topic came up in all the years thereafter, gave me the courage and the confidence to know that I could do this—to continue in a relationship with her that would be full and complete, not lacking one thing.

Her response was the most extravagant expression of love I had ever felt in my life up to that point.

You might be thinking, "I never could have responded like Lana did. I'd be really ticked if I were her, after hearing what you had to say." Believe me, I would think the same thing. But for Lana, her response was as natural as breathing.

It probably didn't hurt that she believed that God had spoken to her on that first night when I gave her that goodnight kiss, and she told her friend that she had just met the man she was going to marry.

After we were married, when she told me about what God had said to her that night, she said she felt it *must* have been God who had spoken to her because of the way the words were phrased when they came into her head: "That's the man *you're* going to marry."

Had it been her own thoughts, she said, she would have said it like this: "That's the man *I'm* going to marry." She truly believed God was speaking to her that night, and those are the words she trusted from that day forward, even when, at times, it looked like marrying me might never happen.

Let me just reiterate how much Lana's response truly overwhelmed me. I was at such a fragile point. I had been wrestling so intensely with my feelings over the monumental decision I was trying to make, so what she said, and what she didn't say, soothed my soul in a way I never could have imagined.

Lana was the kind of friend I needed at that critical juncture in my life, and she continued to be that kind of friend for the rest of her life.

I know that everyone won't have the same reasons for loving their gay friends and relatives as Lana had for loving me. She certainly had a unique role to play in my life.

But what I loved about her response is something that can apply to *anyone*: Lana didn't let the confusion that was going on in *my* mind keep her from seeing me as the person *she* believed me to be.

She loved me. She saw me as a man, fully heterosexual, and fully capable of becoming the husband and father which I eventually became. (In her case, *her* husband and the father of *her* children!)

This is the same thing you can do for your friends or relatives who are struggling with same-sex attractions: *don't let the confusion that may be going on in their minds keep you from seeing them as the people you believe them to be, and who God created them to be.*

While some people might take offense at a statement like this, they shouldn't. Sometimes other people can see in us what we can't see in ourselves.

YOUR RESPONSE

You might feel unqualified to be this kind of person in the lives of your friends or relatives. If so, let me add at this point that Lana didn't have any particular gifting or calling to minister to someone who was struggling with same-sex attractions. She didn't know or suspect that I had even had same-sex attractions until the moment I told her.

Lana didn't have a special "heart" for gays, and she had never experienced same-sex attractions herself. She just loved me, pure and simple.

You might think that you don't have anything to offer to someone with same-sex attractions, but that's *so far from the truth!* If you love someone, if you care about his or her life, you have a tremendous treasure trove to offer to that person! You don't have to have gone through what they're going through to be a huge blessing to them. You don't have to even try to "live in their skin" for a day or two to try to feel what they're feeling. You just have to love them!

You might, in fact, even be repelled by the idea of same-sex attraction. It may be entirely foreign to you like it was to Lana.

If that's you, let me be the first to say I actually think that's okay! There was a time when I was repelled by the idea myself, and I think that was okay, too. In fact, there was a time when I was repelled by the idea of sex in general, and I think *that's* okay!

Why do I think it's okay? Because just like our attractions can serve us well in the right contexts, our repulsions can serve us well in the right contexts, too.

For instance, I believe we're all wired with a certain repulsion to the idea of sex when we're children. If you've ever seen children watch a couple kiss on TV or in person, they'll often look away, saying, "Yuck! I would never want to do that." Any adults in the room might laugh and tell them that they might feel differently when they're older, to which the children protest even more, firmly believing they will never want to do that, because they truly can't imagine it.

I had those same feelings as a pre-pubescent. I couldn't have imagined sex with another person, either. If I were to plot my attractions on the line that I described earlier, I wouldn't have put a point *anywhere* on that line at all.

SENSORS WITHIN US

Why not? I believe it's because God has put sensors within us to warn us about things that may not be good for us—things which could quite likely harm us.

If a person has sex prior to being able to conceive a child, that is, from nature's standpoint for sure, pointless at best and damaging at worst. Our bodies simply aren't created to engage in sex as children. It makes sense to me, then, that God would also hard-wire a response within us that causes us to say, "Yuck!" when approached by others to do things which could potentially harm us.

I don't know if this was true for you, but for me, the first time I learned about what sex really was I was shocked! I couldn't believe my own father and mother had ever done that! But I knew they must have, and more than once, because I knew that my siblings and I all came from them.

I remember talking with another friend my age who had just learned about sex the same day I did. We were both completely repulsed by the idea. Neither of us wanted to even *think* about the fact that our parents had ever done it, and I didn't *consider* the fact that they might *still* be doing it after all those years. It was inconceivable!

It wasn't until I hit puberty that my thoughts on the topic began to change, and I started to actually have any inklings that I might someday want to do that myself. Even then, the idea was still so foreign to me that it scared me quite a bit to think of ever *having* to do it. But like many things in life, what initially repulsed me eventually intrigued me.

It wasn't until college, as I mentioned earlier, that someone seriously approached me about having sex with them—and that someone happened to be a man.

When that happened, there were still some internal hurdles I had to get over, sensors which were going off which I had to ignore, something to which most people could probably relate.

Having kissed only women up to that point, the idea of kissing a man with stubble on his face was more than a little bit awkward. Many people are still at least a little bit squeamish when seeing their first gay kiss, whether on TV or in a movie or in person. There's something about it that, even to me to this day, and even after having been involved in homosexuality myself for several years, still doesn't seem quite right.

I believe this response is okay, too, perhaps even quite "natural." A response like this doesn't mean you love gays *less*—it might actually be a sign of your ability to love them *more*, to truly love them, as you're less likely to ever become sexually or romantically entangled with them yourself.

Like children who are repelled by the idea of sex in general, I can't help but think that these sensors within us regarding homosexuality are built into us by God also, as warnings to strongly consider what we're about to do before we do it. For some people, those God-given lines have been crossed so early and so often that there's no longer any recollection that there were ever any lines in the first place which had been crossed.

But for me, I was fairly aware most every time I crossed such a boundary.

I say all of this to say that *you* can be a loving friend to those with same-sex attractions, whether or not you have a special "heart" for gays, whether or not you've ever had same-sex attractions yourself, and even whether or not you're repulsed by the idea of someone having same-sex attractions.

The fact that you simply love someone who *does* have same-sex attractions qualifies you as one of the best friends to help them through their struggles—like Lana was one of the best friends I could have ever had to help me through mine.

Chapter 6:

The Value Of A Loving God

———— ❖ ————

In which I share why it's helpful to bring people to Jesus, how some friends brought me to Jesus, and the incredible value of having a loving relationship with Him.

———— ❖ ————

There's a story in the Bible of some people who brought their friend to Jesus. Their friend needed a healing touch, both in body and in soul.

Because of their friend's condition, he couldn't get to Jesus on his own. So they carried him. When they finally got to the house where Jesus was speaking, the crowd was so large they couldn't get in. So they went to the roof, created an opening, and lowered their friend down to Jesus.

The Bible says that when Jesus saw *their* faith, He healed him, both in body and in soul.

Wow! Their friend was able to walk home later that day on his own two feet—healed, forgiven, and rejoicing. The story concludes by saying, "Everyone was amazed and gave praise to God. They were filled with awe and said, 'We have seen remarkable things today'" (Luke 5:26).

The truth is, *you* can be this kind of friend for someone you love today. How do I know? Because I had friends who did the same for me.

My friends weren't specifically gifted to help me with what I was needing. They knew I was wrestling with something, but they didn't even know what. They just brought me to Jesus.

Then Jesus did what He does best. He healed me both in body and in soul.

While I was still extremely attracted to Lana at the time—a strong 11 on a 10-point scale—I still saw nothing inherently *wrong* with homosexuality. Although being gay wasn't something I wanted to pursue for myself, I still thought it was quite okay for others to pursue.

I still enjoyed being with my gay friends, often feeling an unspoken, kindred spirit with them. I didn't think that what they were doing or what I had done, was particularly abnormal or abhorrent, just unaccepted. I felt like I understood my gay friends' thoughts, desires, and attractions in a way that most of my ever-straight friends probably never would.

Then three years after walking away from my last gay relationship, I had the most significant encounter with God that I've ever had in my life—and, at its core, it revolved around the issue of homosexuality.

EYE-OPENING WORDS

After graduating from college and going overseas on a short-term stint as a computer consultant, I moved back to the States to take a job in Texas in the computer department of a Fortune 10 corporation. A cousin who lived in that same city invited me to go to church with her, so I went.

Although I had gone to church all my life, I still had some basic questions about the Christian faith—like whether or not Jesus really lived or died or rose again.

I liked Jesus' teachings, and I liked the idea of trying to be a good and decent person. But I couldn't bring myself to believe in Him like some of the people around me seemed to believe in Him.

At my cousin's church, I found a group of people with whom I felt I could truly be honest about my doubts.

One weekend, on a singles' retreat, I shared with a small group of guys that I wasn't sure if I really believed in Jesus or not. One of the guys, astutely picking up on my obvious questions about the faith, invited me to a Bible study with a group of guys that met each week in his home.

This man said they simply read the Bible, talked about what it said, and tried to apply the words they read to their lives. I thought it sounded like a great idea, so the next week I went.

It was in that Bible study that I read for the first time what God had to say about homosexuality.

We were reading the words of the Apostle Paul—words, which I mentioned in Chapter 2, had been written nearly 2,000 years ago and over 5,000 miles away from where I lived.

As I read Paul's words, in the opening passage of this letter he had written to the Christians in Rome, God brought those words to life for me *personally.*

It was as if a light bulb went off in my head. I felt God saying to me, "Eric, I've given you the gift of sex so that you could have an abundant life. But you've used that gift in a way that I never intended—a way that could bring about the very opposite: death."

"Death?" I thought. "Surely not. Surely I couldn't die from anything I've done."

My words sounded vaguely familiar to what the serpent had said to Eve in the Garden of Eden about eating fruit from the tree which God had told her not to eat: "'You will not surely die,' the serpent said to the woman" (Genesis 3:4).

But Eve *did* eat of the deadly fruit, then she handed it to Adam and encouraged him to do the same—just like I had eaten of something that could have killed me and had encouraged others to do the same as well.

"How could I possibly die from *that*?" I wondered. "I was just having fun."

Then I thought of AIDS. I had never been tested for AIDS before. I had never even given it a thought. Suddenly, I was overwhelmed with fear. What if I really *had* contracted a disease for which, at that time, there was no cure and no way to halt its steady march toward death.

I didn't want to die! I wanted to live! And God *wanted* me to live! But what could I do? I couldn't take back what I had done.

Although the men in my Bible study had no idea that I had been involved in homosexuality, they knew I was wrestling with something. So they had brought me to Jesus.

Now Jesus Himself was speaking to me, through the power of the Holy Spirit and through the words of the Bible, which God had inspired the Apostle Paul to write.

As I read those words, I could tell they were the same words that were already written on my heart, only the words I was reading on the pages of my Bible in front of me were written in black and white. The words on my heart had *tried* to warn me whenever I crossed a boundary line that I shouldn't have crossed, not only homosexually with men, but heterosexually with Lana as well.

Yet, I had ignored their warnings. As a result, I was now possibly headed toward my own peril.

As much as I didn't want to die, and as much as I didn't want to believe that what I had done could ever possibly lead to my death, I suddenly felt that if I *were* to die from what I had done, it would be fair.

It wasn't like God hadn't given me warning indicators along the way. It's that I just kept going forward in spite of those warnings. It wouldn't be God's fault for my doing what I knew I shouldn't have done. That fault lay entirely with me.

I had never felt such a heaviness before. I had never felt such a true sorrow for my actions. I tried to see any way out of my predicament, but if there was a way out, I couldn't see it.

How could I take back what I had done? And how could I change the thoughts, feelings, desires, and attractions that I still felt within me?

THE WAY

Then God, in His amazing grace, *showed* me the way!

The very next day, I was reading a passage in the the Bible from the book of Matthew about two blind men who asked Jesus to heal them.

"Have mercy on us," they said to Jesus.

And Jesus, instead of making a paste of mud and putting it on their eyes or telling them to dip in a particular pool of water as He had done with others, simply asked them a question.

Jesus asked, "Do you believe that I am able to do this?" (Matthew 9:28b).

When I read that question, I felt like Jesus was asking me the same question regarding my desire to be healed from my own attractions that could have possibly cost me my life. I sensed very clearly that Jesus was asking me, "Eric, do you believe that I am able to do *this*, too?"

I thought about everything I had ever heard about Jesus: how He healed the sick, walked on water, and raised the dead. I knew that if anyone could do this, Jesus could.

All alone, I reached out my hand toward the sky, and I gave Jesus the same answer that those blind men had given Him. I said, "Yes, Lord, I believe."

In that instant, when I said those words from my heart, Jesus touched me, just like He touched the blind men, and said to me just what He said to them: "According to your faith will it be done to you" (Matthew 9:29).

In that moment, the incredible burden I had felt up to that point—the weight of all that I had done—lifted immediately. Any remaining power that homosexuality still held over my life was broken. *I knew that I knew* that homosexuality would never have a hold on me again.

That night, a friend invited me to a church where I heard a missionary talk about the reason Jesus came to earth: to die for those things we had done wrong in our lives and to break the power that those things held over us. If I were willing to put my full faith and trust in Him, He would give me an abundant life, both here on earth and in heaven forever.

I had never felt, even from Lana, such an overwhelming love as I felt that night. It was astounding. It was wonderful. It was all-encompassing. I thought, "If Jesus was willing to die for me, then I am certainly willing to live for Him."

When I went to bed that night, I climbed onto my bed, got down on my knees, and buried my head in my pillow. Then I cried.

I cried over everything I had done in the past that went against God's plan for my life. I confessed to Him—agreed with Him—that I had made a mess of my life up to that point. I wanted *Him* to take control from that point forward.

I asked Jesus to be my *Lord*, the one who would call the shots from there on out.

For the first time in my life, I truly believed that Jesus was exactly who He said He was. I had done what the Apostle Paul said to do in his letter to the Romans in order to be saved: "That if you confess with your mouth, 'Jesus is Lord,' and believe in your heart that God raised Him from the dead, you will be saved" (Romans 10:9).

The next day I woke up to a whole new life.

A DEFLATED BEACH BALL

Prior to turning my life over to Jesus like this, the battle of trying to keep my homosexual attractions under control was like trying to hold a beach ball underwater. I could do it, but it took a fair amount of effort.

Even though I was deeply in love with Lana, I still had a gravitational pull toward men because I still had a deep, deep need for love and acceptance from them. While Lana was able to meet my needs for feminine intimacy in a way that only a woman could, she wasn't able to meet my needs for male affirmation and acceptance that only a man could.

But here *Jesus* had done it!

The moment I put my faith in Jesus, it was like He walked up with a switchblade in His hand and punctured a hole in that beach ball, once and for all. The beach ball collapsed and sank into the water and down to the sand at my feet, having lost any power it could possibly still hold over my life.

Then Jesus gave me an embrace like no other man could have ever given me.

Everything in my life changed that day, including my thoughts and desires regarding homosexuality. I remember going to lunch soon after with a man who was extremely attractive.

Prior to putting my faith in Christ, I could hardly look at this man when I was with him because I found him so alluring. But when we went to lunch together after coming to Christ, I was able to sit and *fully* enjoy my time with him for the first time, talking and laughing and enjoying him for who he was, a true friend—a true brother in Christ.

I was amazed I could look at him without having any of those unhealthy pulls that had made looking at him so difficult before!

This was remarkable! Jesus had really done it! He had really broken the power that those attractions had held over my life for so long!

When people ask me now if I still have same-sex attractions, I don't mind telling them, "Yes, from time to time, I still do." The difference now is that they no longer have power over my life. They no longer control me. They no longer make me feel like I have to hold those feelings down, like trying to hold a beach ball under water.

I still notice those attractions from time to time, but now it's more like brushing my feet up against that deflated beach ball. Whenever that happens, I just brush it away or step aside.

I was truly a free man—and I still am to this day! Hallelujah!

I could never overstate what Lana did for me, and how her love and her friendship helped to pull me out of homosexuality initially. But I could also never overstate what *Jesus* did for me and how *His* love and *His* friendship dealt a death blow to my same-sex attractions, once and for all.

AN ABUNDANT LIFE

Lana, incidentally, put her faith in Christ around the same time that I did. She, too, had begun reading the Bible on her own for the first time in her life.

In her case, while she had always believed in Jesus and had prayed to Him regularly since she was a little girl, it wasn't until she began reading the Bible for herself as an adult that she realized she had never truly invited Christ be her Lord—letting Him call the shots and following His lead, rather than asking Him to bless whatever activities she had already decided to do.

As we both put our trust in Jesus, Jesus put a deeper love in our hearts for one another as well, eventually leading us to get married and enjoy the fullness of the uninhibited sexual life which God had intended for us all along.

Over the course of the next several years, God gave us a child, then another, then a third and a fourth and a fifth and a sixth! An abundant life! Praise God!

There's much more to my love story with Lana, which I've recorded in my book, *Fifty Shades of Grace,* and which describes in more detail how my thoughts, feelings, desires, and attractions continued to change.

But for the purposes of *this* book, it's enough to say that Lana had given me the fullness of her love, and Jesus had given me the fullness of His—and the change that resulted from experiencing their love was dramatic.

I'm so thankful to them both, as well as to my friends who initially brought me to Jesus, all of which brings us back to the story at the beginning of this chapter about the friends who brought *their* friend to Jesus—and how you can do the same for *your* friends.

YOUR QUALIFICATIONS

You might think you're not qualified to help your gay friends or family members out of homosexuality. The good news is that you don't have to do it on your own!

If you'll keep leading your friends toward Jesus, He'll do the rest! As I said before, God is in the life-changing business. It's one of His specialties.

Think about my cousin who invited me to church. Think about the man at that retreat who invited me to his Bible study. Think about the men in that study who came alongside me to help me read and apply the words of God to my life.

None of these people knew I was wrestling with homosexuality, let alone how to help me through it if they *had* known. But what they *did* know was that Jesus could do anything—absolutely anything. They did what they knew they could do, and they let Jesus do the rest.

The truth is that few people have ever been talked out of homosexuality, but many people have been walked out of it. If you love people, then you have what it takes to bring them through *anything* they might be going through, including this!

To those of you who are straight and have never had a same-sex attraction in your life, let me add this: the fact that you've *never* struggled in this area is actually one of the *best* qualifications for you to truly be of help.

Why? In my own life, what I was seeking in my gay relationships was the affirmation, acceptance, and true love of the people around me. While I found this acceptance to some degree among my gay friends, there was often an underlying motive lurking just beneath the surface. Things weren't always as they appeared.

What I found in this men's Bible study were men who affirmed, accepted, and truly loved me, but who had no interest in me romantically or sexually. This was utterly freeing!

After I put my faith in Christ and told the men in my Bible study about my decision, they wholeheartedly rejoiced with me! In the weeks that followed, they could see the difference it was making in my life, the new sense of purpose my faith in Christ had given me. While they still didn't know about my same-sex attractions nor what Christ had done for me specifically, they rejoiced with me all the same, seeing that I truly was a changed man.

TELLING OTHERS

Shortly after making my decision for Christ, I decided to tell one of the men in my Bible study *specifically* what had happened that caused me to put my faith in Christ.

This man and I worked together at the same company, and we had become particularly good friends during my first year in Texas.

As I was about to tell him the specifics of my story, though, it felt like I was telling Lana all over again. I was scared to death of how he might react. I was afraid that I might lose him as a friend. At the same time, I very much wanted him to know what had really happened deep down inside of me.

And just as it had happened with Lana, when I finally got the words out, my friend didn't freak out, and he didn't back away.

Instead, he stood up and gave me a huge hug.

Although he had never experienced same-sex attractions in all his life, and he didn't have any attractions toward me, he still loved me. He still cared about me. And he continued to be my friend, not only that day, but the next day, and the next, and the next, all the way up to today, over 30 years later.

What my friend did for me by simply listening to me, then standing up and giving me a hug, broke off *years* of feeling like I was second-class among my male peers. It broke off *years* of being ridiculed and feeling unaccepted. It broke off *years* of trying to meet my valid needs for close male friends in invalid ways.

Here was a friend who loved me for who I was, who wasn't fazed by what I had done, and who was willing to keep loving me long into the future.

Little by little, I began sharing my story with others who were close to me: my cousin who had brought me to church; her parents who had been praying for me since the day I arrived in their city; and other men who were also struggling with same-sex attractions who wanted to hear what God had done in my life and how He had done it.

God was so gracious to me, *not* asking me to share my story with the whole world, but letting me know that it was actually okay to *not* share it with the whole world, at least not at that time. In the story in the Bible about the two blind men whom Jesus had healed, I noticed that Jesus told them specifically *not* to tell anyone what He had done for them!

Why not? That didn't sound very evangelistic to me! But that wasn't the right time. Jesus apparently had another time for them to share, which is why their story went on to be recorded in the Bible and has now become part of my own story.

I love the fact that Jesus cares about *us* so much and cares about *others* so much that *He* will guide us regarding when we should share, what we should share, and with whom He wants us to share.

Even Jesus Himself held back from telling His disciples *everything* that was on His heart at times—not because He didn't want them to know, and not because He wouldn't let them know eventually, but because He knew it would be more than they could bear at that time.

At one point, Jesus told His disciples: "I have much more to say to you, more than you can now bear. But when He, the Spirit of truth, comes, He will guide you into all truth. He will not speak on His own; He will speak only what He hears, and He will tell you what is yet to come" (John 16:12-13).

So I simply tried to stay close to Jesus, sharing my story when He prompted me to share. As time went on, I sensed Jesus was prompting me to share more and more.

I was growing stronger in my faith, and I could see how my story was being used in more and more ways and how it could be truly helpful to others.

Two years after I put my faith in Christ, and soon after Lana and I were married, the pastor of the singles' class at the church where we were attending asked if I would be willing to share my story with the whole class, a group of about 200 people. I was nervous, and I shook like a leaf the whole time I was talking. But I could see God working in person after person as I laid out the story of what Jesus had done for me.

At the end of my message, the entire class *stood and cheered.* They were truly touched and deeply filled with faith that God could do anything—absolutely anything.

Their response totally caught me off guard, having just shared with them what was for me the most closely-held secret of my life. They weren't cheering because of my secret, of course, but because of the way God had changed my life and redeemed me from that which could have taken my life had I continued on that path.

Several told me later that they were encouraged by what God had done for me, because it gave them hope that God could do something similar for them, too, no matter what they were facing.

MORE HEALING

After that talk, God continued inviting me to share more often. And as I saw how God was able to use my story for His own glory, I was willing to keep sharing.

I also began to see how sharing my story gave *me* an extra dose of healing that *I* was needing, too. Here I was afraid that by speaking so publicly about what had always been so private, my story would push people away from me even more. Instead, I found that my sharing allowed people the chance to express their love to me in spite of what I had done. Only in God's economy could He bring something so good out of something so bad.

For those of you who are fearful (like I am), to tell others what God has done for you in your life, let me underscore just how much healing God did in my own heart as I shared.

I remember telling my story to one of the straightest guys I've ever known—a big, burly guy who was the head football coach at a local high school. He's a man's man, for sure! And here I was, feeling like God wanted me to tell him that I had been gay.

This man was part of another men's group that I later attended in a small town in Illinois where our family lived after our time in Texas. He and I had become prayer partners, meeting with each other once a week to pray for and encourage one another before going off for the day to our respective jobs.

After a period of meeting like this, I felt I should tell him what God had done for me regarding my same-sex attractions.

I was afraid, once again, of telling someone else what I had done. It was a tense morning for me, as I felt I had so much to lose—so much on the line.

But, as before with Lana and then with my co-worker in Texas, after sharing my story with this man, he stood up, and he, too, gave me a huge bear hug. He cried as he told me he loved me, he appreciated me, and he thanked me for sharing this personal part of my life with him.

He had never had same-sex attractions in his life, either. For me, and because of the way the guys on the football team in my high school had treated me in the past, this coach's hug and his words of affirmation brought me full circle.

It's been over 20 years now since I shared my story with that man, and, interestingly, he's now leading a weekly Bible study with the youth at a new church in another town where we both happen to live—a Bible study which happens to include one of my own teenage sons!

Instead of my story pushing him away as I had feared, this man's heartfelt embrace, not only of me, but of my whole family as well, has continued for more than 20 years.

Can you see how God can use an ever-straight guy who knows little to nothing about homosexuality to minister to a broken guy who is very much in need of his help? It doesn't take much, but it does take something: it takes love—pure, unadulterated, heartfelt love.

If I could do one thing for those struggling with same-sex attractions, it would be to match them all up with others who have never struggled in this area of their lives and ask them to walk alongside one another for a season or two—or for life.

BRINGING YOUR FRIENDS TO JESUS

Just as I could never overstate what Lana has done for me in filling those lonely places in my heart for a soulmate, a helper, a lover, and a daily friend; and just as I could never overstate what Jesus has done for me in filling that God-sized whole in my heart in a way that only He could fill; I could also never overstate what my straight friends have done in terms of filling in those places in my life where I have needed and longed for close friends—friends who could walk alongside me throughout life and who could share a connection with me which is neither romantic nor sexual, but which meets one of my greatest needs that only they can fill.

The *best* thing that Lana and my other friends have done for me over all these years has been to keep pointing me to Jesus—the one who was able to heal me and save me and change me from the inside out.

He's the one who is there for me every night when I go to bed and every morning when I wake up. He's the one who knows what I'm going through every moment of the day, who can rejoice with me when I rejoice, and who can cry with me when I cry.

He's the one who gave me my life from the beginning and who gave me a new life again when I put my faith in Him.

I love the fact that if you don't like the way you were born, you can be born again! Just put your faith in Jesus! Hallelujah!

As Jesus told a man named Nicodemus who came to Him one night: "I tell you the truth, no one can see the kingdom of God unless he is born again.... For God so loved the world that He gave His one and only Son, that whoever believes in Him shall not perish but have eternal life" (John 3:3 and 3:16).

Bring your friends to Jesus. You might not know what they need, but He does. You might not be able to heal them, but He can. Keep doing what you can, and keep trusting Him to do the rest.

Study Guides For Chapters 5 & 6

STUDY GUIDE FOR CHAPTER 5: "THE VALUE OF A LOVING FRIEND"

CHAPTER SUMMARY

The author says he would plot his own attractions on a scale of 0 to 10 at three different places along that continuum over time:

- as a teenager, at a 7 or 8, strongly leaning toward heterosexuality, even though he had never engaged in sex at that time,
- in his early 20's, at a 2 or 3, strongly leaning toward homosexuality, after having had his first and subsequent sexual interactions with men,
- and in his mid-20's, at a 10+, leaning overwhelmingly toward heterosexuality, after having an intimate relationship with the woman who eventually became his wife.

In the 30 years since he came out of homosexuality, he has never gone back.

After telling his girlfriend about his same-sex attractions, she responded by saying that she loved him still and was willing to walk with him through this as well. She became one of his strongest supporters in helping him to come out of homosexuality, simply by loving him through it. He says that she:

- had no special "heart" for gays,
- had never experienced same-sex attractions herself,
- and didn't let the confusion that was going on in *his* mind keep her from seeing him as the person *she* believed him to be, and the person she believed *God* had created him to be.

You can do the same for those you love.

The author says that people can help gays tremendously, even if they might be squeamish about the idea of homosexuality. The fact that someone has no same-sex attractions qualifies them even more to truly love those who do, giving them their wholehearted affection without having any romantic or sexual expectations.

QUESTIONS FOR REFLECTION & DISCUSSION

Read John 3:17. Why do you think the response of the author's girlfriend was so helpful to him in his own journey?

Why is it important to not let the confusion going on inside someone else's head keep you from seeing them as you believe them to be and as you believe God created them to be?

Read Proverbs 25:11. Before reading this chapter, how might you have responded if someone you loved told you they were gay? After reading this chapter, how might you wish you would be able to respond? (And if someone you love has already told you they were gay, how did you respond, and how might you wish you would have responded?)

Can you understand why the author's feelings of attraction shifted over time from mostly straight to mostly gay, after his first intimate encounters with men, and later after having his first intimate encounter with a woman? What role do you think "valid needs" played in his attractions in each of those scenarios and in each of those shifts in his feelings?

Consider the statement: "Sex is a wonderful *extension* of intimacy, but as a *substitute*, it will never compare." When people with same-sex attractions "just try" having sex with someone of the opposite sex, why might such encounters often tend to fall flat?

How can someone who has never experienced same-sex attractions be especially helpful to someone who *has* had such attractions? What can someone offer to others even if they might not have a special "heart" for gays—or might even be repelled by the idea of homosexuality?

STUDY GUIDE FOR CHAPTER 6: "THE VALUE OF A LOVING GOD"

CHAPTER SUMMARY

The Bible tells the story of some friends who brought their friend to Jesus to be healed. We can learn three things from this story:

- when Jesus saw *their* faith, He healed their friend in body and soul,
- while *you* might not know what your friends really need, Jesus does,
- and if you'll do what you can do—bring your friends to Jesus—He'll do what He can do!

The author shares how some friends brought *him* to Jesus, not even knowing that he was struggling with homosexual feelings, yet knowing he was struggling with something. Jesus then healed the author in body and soul.

The author describes how it happened like this:

- while reading the Bible, he realized that he had done something which could have killed him,
- he repented of that which he had done and was set free from ever again having his same-sex attractions control his life,
- and he describes the change as going from trying to hold a beach ball under water to having Jesus sink that ball by taking a switch blade to it, defeating any ability the ball had to rise again of its own accord.

The author says he's thankful to his friends for doing what they could do and thankful to Jesus for doing what He could do. He encourages others to bring their friends to Jesus, realizing that his own ongoing relationship with Jesus has brought him the most healing of all.

QUESTIONS FOR REFLECTION & DISCUSSION

Read Luke 5:17-26. What is it about the faith of the friends that might have so moved the heart of Jesus?

Read Matthew 9:27-31. Why do you think Jesus asked the blind men if they *believed* He could heal them? According to Jesus, what role did their faith in Him play in their healing? According to the author, what role did his faith in Jesus play in his healing?

Read Romans 10:8-10. According to this passage, what does it take to be saved? What happened for the author when he declared that Jesus was his Lord and believed in his heart that God raised Him from the dead?

Read John 16:12-13. Why did Jesus not always share the fullness of what He *could* have shared with His disciples? What wisdom might there have been for the author to not share the fullness of what he might have shared about his testimony with others? How did that wisdom bring relief to him as well?

In what ways could you "bring your friends to Jesus"? What kinds of activities could you invite them to or what kinds of things could you do yourself to help introduce them to Him?

The author uses the analogy of holding a beach ball underwater to describe how his attractions once had a hold on his life. Have you ever felt a similar hold on some area of your life? What kind of relief did it bring, or would it bring, if Jesus were to take a switchblade to that beach ball, once and for all? Would you be willing to invite Jesus to do that?

In what ways did the author realize that sharing his story, on select occasions and with select people, brought even more healing to him in his own life? In what ways could these thoughts apply to you as you consider sharing your own story?

Chapter 7:

The Value Of A Loving Church

———— ❖ ————

In which I share how the church has helped
me in this area of my life—including my local
church, the church beyond the walls of my
church, and the church throughout history.

———— ❖ ————

Some people ask: "What about the church's abysmal response to
this issue? Don't you think it's been horrific?"

To that, I have to ask, "What has been your *personal* experience with
the church on this issue?" I sincerely want to know. Because while I've
heard horror stories of how some churches have talked about this
issue, I've only heard those stories in news accounts or in magazines or
on TV shows.

I have never been part of a church in my whole life where I have
felt anything but loved, accepted, cared for, respected, and treated with
heartfelt compassion on this issue—even when I was involved in
homosexuality.

I've been in church all my life, for over five decades now, in
churches of different sizes, different denominations, and different
cities. And in all my years of attending those churches, week after week
after week for over 50 years, I have never once heard a sermon or a
teaching that has made me personally feel unwelcome, unappreciated,
uncared for, or unwanted.

Not once have I felt demeaned, reproached, humiliated, or
threatened. In fact, I have found the exact opposite. The leaders and
people in those churches have been welcoming, loving, caring,
thoughtful, interested, and kind. As I've shared my honest feelings with
people about my own same-sex attractions, whether one-on-one or

within small groups or from the stage, I have felt honored, accepted, and respected.

I have been hugged more times than I could possibly count, by men and woman across the board, from a wide range of backgrounds, shapes, and sizes (including burly football coaches). The love and acceptance which Christians have shown to me has, in so many settings, significantly helped to further my own healing throughout this journey. I have found the church to be a refuge, a sanctuary, and a place of healing and acceptance.

It is "out there," out in "the world"—whether in gym classes or public spaces or secular settings—where I have felt vilified, mistreated, disrespected, threatened, bullied, shamed, and demeaned. It is out there, in the world, where I have felt rejected, cast out, humiliated, and unappreciated. It is out there that I have been called gay, sissy, faggot, queer, and [expletive deleted] homo—but never, ever, not once, in the church.

Before I moved to Texas, I read an article in a national news magazine about a church in that state. The article described what that church thought about gays and would do to gays if any came to that church.

I remember thinking, "Wow! I don't see how I could ever live in Texas. That would be horrible!"

But when I got a job offer from a company in Texas and *did* move there, what I found within the church where I *did* attend were the kindest, most helpful group of guys who loved me and cared for me like I've never been loved or cared for before.

That church was the first setting in my life where I felt so appreciated for my gifts and talents and unique wiring—and this coming from people who *didn't* want to have sex with me! Their genuine affection won me over and opened my heart to Christ, changing the rest of my life.

Some of the men from that church went on to become some of my best, life-long friends, standing up for me at my wedding and still supporting me and my family and my ministry to this day. But had I taken my queues from what I had read in that national news magazine, I never would have even moved to Texas.

So my first question to those who think the church has responded abysmally to people with same-sex attractions is to ask what their *personal* experience has been.

MY EXPERIENCE IN THE CHURCH

Perhaps my experience is a testimony to the *types of churches* of which I've chosen to be a part. But I've been involved with a wide variety of churches over the years, not just one size or flavor. The churches have ranged in size from a few dozen members to several thousand members and have crossed various theological lines from mainline and evangelical to non-denominational and charismatic.

Or perhaps my experience is a testimony to the way I happen to *personally react* to the things I hear spoken in the church. While there have been times when I've disagreed with a speaker or a leader on a topic, I've tended to let those bits slide right off, as I can usually hear the hearts of the people behind their words.

So I'm not too offended by what people say in the churches where I attend, because I know and believe they are *trying* to do the right thing; they're *trying* to live like Christ as fully as they can. And honestly, even though I have some very strong beliefs on certain topics, I still rarely hear things in a church setting with which I disagree to the point of anger or rage or feeling my own thoughts or opinions have been unduly denigrated.

Have I been hurt by the church at times? Yes. Do I have some "bad church stories" of my own where people have treated me in ways that I felt wasn't particularly Christian, ways which have indeed wounded me, sometimes very deeply? Yes. But never in a way that has disparaged homosexuality.

Even when I *was* involved in homosexuality in college, I still attended church. I remember hearing a sermon on sex and thinking afterward, "I have some different thoughts on that topic." But I wasn't hurt or offended by what they said. I respected what was said, because I could hear the heart of the speaker for the hearts of those of us in the congregation.

MY EXPERIENCE ONLINE

Some people might think that I must have had a very limited exposure to churches if I've not run across the mean-spiritedness of what they have perceived from the church. But they would be mistaken.

I've run an online ministry for over 20 years which now reaches nearly 40,000 people a day, six days a week, in over 160 countries. From time to time, I'll write about the topic of homosexuality, including my own testimony about how Christ has changed my life.

In more than 20 years of writing and speaking and talking about this topic as part of my ministry, I've only had a handful of people ever respond in a negative way, and those responses have not once come from people who say they hate gays, but only from people who say they love gays, who say they love diversity, and who say they want everyone to be treated with tolerance and respect!

It is only from these, the self-proclaimed, most "tolerant" group of Christians, that I have ever heard anything hateful or mean-spirited toward me or my message regarding this issue. It always strikes me as ironic that those who love the idea of tolerance the most seem to show it the least to those who happen to disagree with them.

I cannot think of one person—not one—in all my years of ministry in this area, who has ever written to me and made me feel condemned or belittled for having shared my experiences with same-sex attractions. And in case you think my subscribers are all just like-minded citizens in the kingdom of God, and perhaps I must just be preaching to my own particular choir, believe me, I'm not! My subscribers are made up of Christians and non-Christians from as many denominations as there could possibly be, located in countries all over the world.

I hear from people regularly about things we've written or sent out with which they *strongly* disagree. They certainly don't hold back their thoughts if they think a quote or a paragraph is out of line with their personal beliefs or theologies, or if an apostrophe or a comma is out of place!

Yet I can't remember hearing even one comment from any Christian regarding anything I've written in regards to homosexuality that has been mean-spirited in regards to my own feelings of having experienced same-sex attractions.

On the contrary, people have been inspired by the stories they've heard, often responding by pouring out the details of their own lives or the lives of those they love, and asking for encouragement through whatever they're facing. People often genuinely want to hear more, much more, about whatever I can tell them related to this topic.

Or perhaps my experience is a testimony to the *way* I present what I'm sharing. Or perhaps it's a testimony to *God's hand of protection* over me in these past 20 years of ministry. Or perhaps it's a combination of *all these things* that I've mentioned.

But to say the *church* has treated gays abysmally or has not been honoring or compassionate toward those who are experiencing same-sex attractions has simply not been my experience, whether it's churches in which I've been involved up here in Illinois, churches in which I've been involved deep in the heart of Texas, or people in churches all around the world to whom I minister daily.

As for the pastors that I've been honored to listen to and learn from week after week, not one of them has *ever* responded in hate or wickedness or bigotry after hearing my story of experiencing same-sex attractions. Pastors have only responded in love and graciousness and appreciation for what I've experienced.

I can think of at least a dozen pastors and leaders at my current church of over 5,000 members who know my story and who regularly greet me with huge hugs, great love, and tremendous respect, not just when I share my story of how God has changed my life, but also when I share my ongoing thoughts and feelings regarding my same-sex attractions.

The small groups in which I have been involved have all done likewise, allowing me to talk openly about my experiences, which often results in others opening up about their own struggles in other arenas of their lives.

YOUR EXPERIENCE

Perhaps you're reading what I'm saying here about the church and this *hasn't* been your experience. If so, I am so sorry, so very sorry. As Christians, we ought to be the most loving ambassadors for the most loving Man who has ever walked the earth.

When I find that we're not acting that way, I'm deeply saddened. I could appeal to the fact that we're all fallen in nature, that none of us is perfect, but that doesn't excuse us for not doing our best to make things right with those we've offended.

If you and I were together in person, I would ask you to share with me what your experience with the church has been, and I would gladly apologize on behalf of my brothers and sisters in Christ for any offenses that have been committed against you. I've done so before and I would do so again.

But after having had that conversation, I would also ask you to tell me what your experiences have been "out there," out in "the world" and then compare them to your experiences in the church.

If, by comparison, your church *has* treated you less lovingly than the way the world has treated you, then I would suggest, as kindly as I could, that you find another church—and not just one that is gay affirming, because I can assure you that you are *not* getting the fullness of what Christ and His soon-to-be-bride, the church, have to offer you. You are *not* getting that which is available to you in thousands of churches throughout the world, churches which are made up of fallen people just like you and me, but whose hearts are truly set on trying to be like Jesus as best as they can be.

Some churches, and by "some," from my experience, I mean truly very few, are frequently featured in news stories as being particularly hate filled and repugnant on this issue.

Those churches are rightly and roundly denounced by Christian viewers of those stories as strongly as they are denounced by secular viewers. Yet even after those churches have been strongly denounced, the media still portrays those churches, on a regular basis, as being somehow representative of most churches everywhere. They are not.

In contrast, I have seen churches which have shown incredible respect and kindness to gays who have come to those churches, not to mention at gay pride parades and celebrations of diversity, where church members hand out water bottles, express their love, and engage in polite and civil discussions with those in attendance. I've seen church members do this in settings where even gays denounce some of the lurid activities in which their fellow gays are engaging publicly in front of children and families.

I've found Christians to be among the most loving, accepting, and affirming groups of people in the world, especially when compared with some of the other major religions today in which homosexuality is still punishable by death. And in all my years of attending Christian churches, I have never once heard any leader in any of those churches call for the death of homosexuals, *or anything less than complete honor, love, and respect* to be shown toward those who are experiencing same-sex attractions.

Having said all of that, for me to say that my experience in the church speaks for *all* people who have *ever* had same-sex attractions would be like asking someone from America to describe what it's like for *everyone* who has grown up in America. It just isn't possible!

All of us have such different personalities, backgrounds, stories, giftings, limitations, and so on that it would be impossible to use one example of one person like me to categorize everyone who experiences same-sex attractions.

Yet, whenever I hear someone talk about how abysmally the church has responded to this issue, this is why I like to ask what their own personal experience has been, because it is truly so foreign to my own. And more often than not, when I ask people this question, they *don't* have specific stories to tell me from their own experience, but rather are repeating stories they've heard from others, often from media reports featuring some of the few churches I've mentioned earlier which nearly all other Christians denounce as well.

I've seen the same thing happen in regards to issues besides homosexuality. Back when I first went into ministry, some major sex scandals rocked the Christian world. I commented to one of the leaders at my church that it seemed like *every pastor* was having an affair. To which he replied, "Oh, I know lots of pastors who have never had affairs."

He was right, and his words helped me to recalibrate my thinking. While there *were* a few very high-profile cases, when I took the time to think through the various pastors that I had known personally over the years, I realized that those few high-profile cases I saw in the news were in the minority.

Although some stories naturally grab the national headlines, the *reason* they grab headlines is not because they are the norm, but because they are precisely the opposite: they grab headlines because they are *not* the norm.

THE BROADER CHURCH

I've shared several stories with you already about the everyday help which people in local churches have given me regarding this issue, including my heterosexual friends I've made in those churches I've attended who have come alongside me, rather than pushing me away.

Let me add to those stories two more, about the broader church and the historical church, which will help you understand just how valuable the church has been to me and to many others, especially at some critical junctures in my journey.

After sharing my testimony with the singles' class at my church in Texas, a woman came up to me and told me about a conference for people who were wrestling with same-sex attractions.

She thought I should check out this conference sometime, but to be honest, I didn't really want to go. Nothing sounded worse than getting together with a bunch of people who had same-sex attractions, because *everyone* there would know *why* I was there! I may as well wear a badge saying, "Yes, I've struggled with same-sex attractions!"

But a few months later, a friend of mine asked if I would be interested in going to this conference with him. He thought it would be helpful in his struggles, so I decided to go, both for his sake and to check out the conference as this woman had suggested.

My desires and attractions for Lana at this time were off the charts as usual, and I was thoroughly enjoying my friendships with several straight, male friends. I wasn't wrestling with any specific issue when I went to the conference, but I did have one question on my heart that I wondered if God could answer for me.

I wondered if there might still be something I was missing in all of this, some critical piece of information that I might have overlooked which someday could come back to haunt me, wrecking my marriage or my family or my life. I didn't think there was, but I didn't want to be blindsided, either, so I thought it would be a good idea to learn all I could learn about this topic from those who had been there before and who had dealt with it over the years.

So I went to the conference. After getting over the initial awkwardness of literally putting a name tag on my chest with the conference logo on it (there it was: my badge saying, "Yes, I've struggled with same-sex attractions!"), I found the whole thing to be amazing.

Here were over 1,000 people who had experienced the same thing that I had experienced! Many of them had already found a way out of it through the power of Christ and were now at various stages of walking out their freedom. Some had just put their faith in Christ and wanted to know what to do next. Others had been walking in complete freedom for 20, 30, and 40 years or more. I had rarely, at that time, come across people who had had a similar experience to what I had had. And here were over 1,000 such people in one place!

I went to session after session, listening to speaker after speaker who confirmed what I had experienced and I had come to believe to be true. It was fascinating!

GOD'S ANSWER TO MY QUESTION

One night during worship, while I was praising God for this gathering of Christians and asking Him what He thought about my question (that is, if there were anything more I needed to know about this issue so it wouldn't come up and later wreck me or my family or my life), a man standing and worshipping next to me, whom I had never met before, turned to me and said: "You will *never* go back to what you once were. You will *never, never, never, never, never* go back."

I was stunned. He could have said those words to anyone at that conference and they could have been helpful, but to me, because this was the exact question that was on my heart for God that week, I couldn't help but pay attention.

What he said next was even more astounding. He said: "Man will give you many opportunities. Don't take them. Take only the ones God gives you. Satan doesn't need to get you to sin in order to keep you from doing God's will for your life. All he has to do is get you to do things other than what *God* wants you to do—even if those other things may be good and godly in and of themselves."

This man's words sank deep into the core of my being.

In those few moments, I dropped any worry that I would ever go back to homosexuality or that it would somehow wreck me or my family or my life.

It's not that I felt immune to temptation, and it's not that I felt I could suddenly let down my guard so much so that I would never have to give it another thought again. But what it *did* do was to help me shift my focus from worrying if something regarding this issue might be lurking around the corner to instead focusing on what I believed God was putting on my heart to do.

After the last session on the last day of the conference, I was walking across campus back to the dorm where I was staying when a car drove by with a couple of guys in it. One of the guys, who apparently had heard that this conference had something to do with homosexuality, leaned out the passenger-side window and yelled at me: "Die, you [expletive deleted] faggot!"

As they drove off at full speed, I burst out laughing! Even though I was wearing a name badge that said, in effect, "I've struggled with same-sex attractions!" I felt like I was the furthest from being gay that I had ever felt in my entire life!

God had done such a remarkable work in my life, and during that week, that my only response to his outburst was to burst out laughing myself! (And, as you might notice, the man who said this to me was not someone within the church, but rather someone "out there," out in "the world." It was the Christians, those within the church, who had put on this conference to help those who wanted the help.)

I found this gathering of Christians to be so hel[
myself but also for my friend and several others with
to converse during the week, that I went back again se
in future years as a speaker on various topics.

I had discovered that the broader church *was* doing its job of loving
God and loving gays—and I was happy to join them in their work.

THE HISTORICAL CHURCH

The other story I'd like to share is about how the *historical* church
has helped me in this area of my life.

I didn't know, for instance, until after I had put my faith in Christ,
that God had also set *others* free from this very same issue in the
churches back then—back in the days soon after Jesus had lived and
died and rose again.

As I continued reading the Bible, I discovered that there had been
people in the church in Corinth, Greece, who had been involved in
homosexuality and whose lives had been transformed by the power of
the Holy Spirit.

The same Apostle Paul who wrote the letter to the Christians in
Rome also wrote a letter to the Christians in Corinth around the years
A.D. 53-57, a mere 20-22 years after Jesus was doing His public
ministry on earth. (Jesus was crucified in A.D. 33.)

In Paul's letter to the Corinthians, he says that some of the people
in that church had been involved in homosexuality, among other things,
then added: "And that is what some of you *were*. But you were washed,
you were sanctified, you were justified in the name of the Lord Jesus
Christ and by the Spirit of our God" (1 Corinthians 6:11, *italics mine*).

That one little word, *were*, is what struck me the most the day that I
first read that passage. Here were people living nearly 2,000 years ago
who had experienced what I had experienced, had been involved in
homosexuality, and then had been pulled out of it in the name of Jesus
Christ and by the power of His Holy Spirit!

If you think I was amazed to find 1,000 people at those conferences
who had all been through what I had been through, you can imagine
my amazement to learn that there were people living in the days just

...er Jesus lived and died and rose again who had also experienced the same thing!!!

I realized that what I had experienced was clearly not something new which is taking place only now in the 20th and 21st centuries. What I had dealt with was something that people had been dealing with for thousands of years.

As I've continued reading the Bible, I've learned that homosexuality was discussed as far back as the days of Abraham, some 4,000 years ago (see Genesis 18:16-19:29).

It was discussed again in the days of Moses, when God gave Moses instructions about how we should live, some 3,300 years ago (see Leviticus 18:22 and 20:13).

And homosexuality was discussed again in the years just following Christ's ministry here on the earth, some 2,000 years ago (see 1 Corinthians 6:9-11).

All this is to say that God is not surprised by homosexuality! It's not something that has suddenly sprung up in my lifetime!

God is not surprised that people would be tempted by it. In fact, that's *why* He addresses it in the Bible!

God doesn't address things in the Bible that He *doesn't* think people would be tempted to do, but rather, He addresses things that He *knows* we'll be tempted to do. And on this topic in particular, God has expressed His warnings to us as clearly as He possibly could.

Yet, I have seen person after person try to take those clear and explicit warnings and do some mental and theological gymnastics to make it sound like God actually *wanted* us to engage in homosexuality.

I get it. I understand their readings of those passages, and I've read their arguments in favor of it. But for me, every one of those arguments simply falls flat. Why? Because I've tried to imagine what words God *could* have used which would have been any more clear or any stronger than the ones He has *already* used.

If the words in the Bible on this issue aren't clear to people, then what words would be? What words would people *want* God to have said if He truly didn't want them to engage in homosexuality? (And what words would *you* want Him to say?)

When I've looked through any of the Bible passages I've referenced on the previous pages, I've found that the words used in those passages are stronger than any that I could have come up with myself!

I'm not saying that there might not be various ways of interpreting the words that we have in the Bible. What I am saying is that I would have a hard time coming up with any words that could be any stronger or more clear.

From everything I've read in the Bible, and from all the discussions I've ever heard about everything that I've read, I've been encouraged, over and over, that the life-changing experience that I've had with Christ in this area is something that has happened to many others as well.

I'm also encouraged that people *can* change, *have* changed for thousands of years, and *still* change today, just like I have changed and hundreds of others have changed with whom I have individually met, and thousands beyond that whom I have seen in conferences I have attended.

Why are we surprised, then, to learn that the Spirit of Christ still changes people today as He was clearly changing people nearly 2,000 years ago? The words of the Apostle Paul to the Corinthians are like music to my ears: "And that is what some of you *were*."

Far from having an abysmal record in its treatment of gays, the church, in my experience, has had an amazing record.

I've found love and support in my local church, in the broader church beyond the walls of my church, and in the church throughout history.

No wonder Jesus loves the church so much. No wonder He looks forward to one day joining together with the church, His bride, at the ultimate wedding feast—the wedding supper of the Lamb (see Ephesians 5:31-32, Revelation 19:7, 21:2, and 21:9)

Chapter 8:

A Few Words About Temptation

———— ◆ ————

In which I share why our temptations don't define us, how our attractions can be cooled or fueled, and why we celebrate the 4th of July instead of the Treaty of Versailles.

———— ◆ ————

As I mentioned earlier, when people ask me, "Are you still attracted to men?" I don't mind answering them honestly, "Yes. Yes, I am."

But there's a follow-up question I wish they would ask, for the answer to *that* question is even more significant: "Do those attractions still control your actions?" My answer to that question is a resounding, "No. No, they don't."

And while it may seem like I'm splitting hairs between those two questions and answers, the difference between them is like the difference between night and day.

When God transformed my life, He didn't just change me from a caterpillar into a better caterpillar. He gave me wings so I could fly. He changed me into a whole new creation. As the Bible says: "Therefore, if anyone is in Christ, he is a new creation; the old has gone, the new has come!" (2 Corinthians 5:17).

While I'm still the same person in some ways, I'm an entirely new creation in others.

One of the main reasons I wrote a more intimate book of my testimony a few years ago was to describe, in detail, just how much God had changed my life in the areas of my thoughts and feelings, my desires and attractions. The book was to let people know that real-life change is possible, and that it's not just a cosmetic change, but a complete overhaul of our entire beings.

I also wrote that book to whet people's appetites for *more*, to let them know that if they will let go of their old life, even with all the pleasures and relief from pain that it may offer, that God can give them a whole new life that offers *even more*. I would never recommend that someone follow the path that I have followed if I didn't believe wholeheartedly that it would go better for them in the long run, both here on earth and in heaven forever.

THERE'S *MORE*

I knew a man who, when he first become a Christian, went to a local church. That church was dull. Dry. Boring. Nothing ever happened. The Spirit never flowed.

This man had been so excited to give his life to Jesus, but when he went to this church, he was utterly disappointed. As he looked around one day, he said, "I gave up drugs for THIS?!?"

He knew there had to be *more*. He knew there had to be *more to the abundant life that Jesus had offered to him than what he was experiencing.*

So he pressed on with God, finally going to another church and finding exactly what he was looking for—the abundant life that had been waiting for him all along! This *was* better than the drugs he had given up! Way better! He went on to become a pastor and started more life-giving churches all over the world.

But if I were advising him back in those early days, and his first church experience was truly an indicator of what his new life in Christ was going to look like forever, then I would have been the first to tell him—emphatically—"Go back to drugs!"

I've said as much to a few people who have come to me saying they believe God *made* them gay, yet God doesn't want them to act on the way He made them—that they were destined to live the rest of their lives in frustration and heartache. I've said to them, "If you really believe God *made* you this way, yet He wants you to live the rest of your life frustrated because you'll never be able to act on the way He *made* you, then let me be the first to say, emphatically, 'Go for homosexuality, and go for it with gusto!'"

But I *don't* encourage people to do that, because I *don't* believe God made *anyone* gay, only to frustrate them by the way He made them for the rest of their lives.

I believe there is something else that is holding people back from experiencing the abundant life for which God created them to live. I've also found that many people *do* believe in their hearts that this *isn't* the way God made them, even though they might not be able to find any other way to explain what they're feeling. They just don't see any other options. They feel trapped, in a cage, with no apparent way out.

My desire is to help them figure it out, to explore what God *really* wants them to do, and to give them hope that God *truly does have something more in store for them,* regardless of whether or not they ever get married to someone of the opposite sex.

Jesus didn't promise us an abundant life only to snatch it away from us once we put our faith in Him. While it may *feel* like that at times, that's *not* the truth, and it *won't* feel like that forever.

My encouragement to those who are frustrated and longing for *more* is to keep asking, keep seeking, and keep knocking, for *more will come.*

These aren't just my words of encouragement. They're *His.* Jesus said, "Ask and it will be given to you; seek and you will find; knock and the door will be opened to you. For everyone who asks receives; he who seeks finds; and to him who knocks, the door will be opened" (Matthew 7:7-8).

When Jesus said, "I have come that they may have life, and have it to the full" (John 10:10), He made His promise to all of us who have been willing to put our faith in Him.

What that "full life" will look like will be different in every person's case, and only Jesus Himself knows the full extent of what it might mean for us. But I am confident that God will bring about His fullness of life to every one of us as surely as the sun will rise again tomorrow. God *really does* want all of us to experience the fullest life possible.

OUR RESPONSE-ABILITY

We may not get to choose our feelings, but we do get to choose what we do with our feelings. We do get to choose whether we will cool our feelings or fuel our feelings. We do get to choose whether we will act on our feelings or not act on our feelings.

And what we choose to do with our feelings will, in large measure, determine what kind of experience we will have in these lives that God has given us. How we respond to our feelings is our response-ability.

I know what it's like to be in love with someone deeply, yet not be able to satisfy that love. I know what it's like to have little pink hearts floating over my head whenever I've thought of someone special, but not being able to act on those feelings.

I know what it's like to have my heart lunge out of my chest, yet be unable to retrieve it and stuff it back inside me when I can't express my love in the way that I've wanted to express it.

But I also know what it's like to finally be able to put those desires to rest, to lay them at the feet of Jesus so completely that they no longer cause me the heartache and turmoil and pain of lovesickness anymore.

This doesn't mean that I haven't sometimes tried to breathe life back into my feelings after I've laid them down, wanting to pick up the phone or send a note "just to keep in touch." But I've noticed that whenever I've tried to do one of those "harmless" little things, my heart lunges out of my chest again, and it takes a fair amount of time and effort to put it back in. Then I've gone right back to where I had started.

I've learned that when this happens, the best thing I can do is to put down the phone or not send the note. I've had to recognize that my motives aren't right. My intentions aren't pure.

I know that my feelings will lead me to disappointment if I continue to follow them, because I can never follow through on them in the way that I had hoped. This kind of *heart lunge* is a giveaway for me that my attractions are bordering on dangerous.

Regarding same-sex attractions, to the extent that they are simply attractions, simply an awareness that there's something attractive about someone else, that's not a problem.

The problem comes when our hearts begin lunging toward someone as well. That's when our feelings become dangerous. That's when we need to pull back. That's when we need to figure out what we're really feeling and why.

Then, if after learning that what we're feeling is based on a valid need, we can explore ways of meeting that valid need in a *valid* way rather than an invalid way. If we learn that what we're feeling is *not* tied to a valid need or that this is *not* a valid way to meet that need, then the best thing for us to do is to "leave 'em there." To keep on walking. To turn around and go the other way, giving our hearts time to cool down.

I've found that this simple advice, to say to myself, "Leave 'em there," and keep on walking, not looking back, is amazingly effective. It cancels out those heart pangs that people so often experience in life.

When I tell people that I still have same-sex attractions, what I'm saying is, "Yes, I still recognize whether or not a person is attractive to me." But the vast majority of the time, those attractions are simply *recognitions* of attraction. There is no heart lunge contained within them.

My heart stays fully in my chest. There's no heartache, no longing to take hold of something that I feel is being painfully or unfairly held back from me.

Even when I *do* feel my heart lunging inappropriately toward someone, the simple awareness of it, and the realization that I simply *cannot* act on it for a whole host of reasons, helps me to keep my heart in check—then my heart quickly retracts back into my chest.

GUARDING OUR HEARTS

To me, this is what King Solomon encouraged us to do when he said, "Above all else, guard your heart, for it is the wellspring of life" (Proverbs 4:23).

All too often, we tend to let down the walls of our hearts instead, exposing them fully to the pain which naturally results from not being able to have that for which our hearts are lunging.

What I'm trying to express here is that there's a difference in the way we *experience* our attractions. Our attractions can remain simply attractions, or they can become temptations—and more than that, longings or yearnings which become extremely painful the longer they go unfulfilled.

When my wife died, the pain which I experienced soon afterward was unbelievably intense. Lana had just been there with me only a few days before, lying on our bed next to me, with her head on her pillow and looking at me with her eyes that were so fully alive.

Then, a day came when she was no longer there. My heart longed to be with her, *yearned* to be with her, but I knew it I would never again be able to be with her in person this side of heaven.

Knowing that I would never again fulfill that longing of my heart here on earth, that heart *lunging*, the pain that resulted was as intense as any physical pain I had ever endured.

Yet, as time went on, I found that I was finally able to keep my heart in my chest. I finally came to terms with the fact that my longings for her were simply never going to be fulfilled.

I had reached a particular point in my grief which I later read about in a book by Harold Ivan Smith, called *Decembered Grief.* He quoted a woman who had also reached this point, saying:

"It has taken me many months to get to the point where I can say, 'All right, the future is not going to be what you thought it was. It's gone, and you're not going to have it. You just will not have it. Your future went with him. Now you've got to build a new one.'"

For me, I had to accept the fact that my wife was gone, too, and she wasn't coming back.

When I came to that realization, the pain in my heart diminished greatly. Yes, I would have still *loved* to be with her, to hold her close, and to look deeply into her eyes. But my longing was no longer accompanied by the same kind of pain.

C.S. Lewis describes the difference between these two types of longings, these two types of yearnings, in his book *Out of a Silent Planet.* Lewis wrote that there were two words in the language of the creatures on his fictional planet that meant to long or to yearn, but that the creatures drew a sharp distinction, even an opposition, between them, saying that "everyone would *long* for it (*wondelone*), but no one in his senses *could long* for it (*hluntheline*)."

It's a subtle distinction, but a distinction that makes an important difference in terms of its practical impact on our lives. It's the difference between remembering my wife with pain and heartache versus remembering her with fondness and affection.

My heart-lunging pain would only occur when I still held out hope that somehow what I desired was a real, even if remote, possibility. But once I came to terms with the fact that there was no longer any real or even remote possibility of fulfilling my longing, then the painful part of that longing ceased as well.

Fulfilling my longings in that way was simply not an option, in any sense, remote or otherwise, and my heart stayed fully in its chest.

COOLING OUR DESIRES

To put it another way, there are times when I have passed by someone smoking a cigarette, and even though I've never smoked, I will sometimes breathe in that smoke and think, "Ah, that smells *really* good."

As strange as that might seem to some people, since I've never smoked, I still recognize something alluring about the smell, whether it reminds me of a campfire as a kid, or it stimulates something within me that is pleasurable, I don't really know. (But there it is, another true confession.)

This happened to me again recently. I was walking past a man who was smoking outside of a building where I had been shopping.

The man apologized for smoking in front of me as I walked by. I told him it wasn't a problem, and that even though I had never smoked, I still enjoyed the smell at times.

Now I'm not tempted to smoke. I have no desire to put something within me that could intentionally cause my demise. But I can still recognize the attraction that it holds out to me, and I can see why it holds out an attraction to others, including this man.

Had I grown up in a different environment, or been exposed to different life situations, I could have easily been standing there smoking right along with him. But because I didn't, and because I don't plan on ever satisfying that particular desire, my heart never *lunges* toward the idea of smoking.

I'm able to keep walking straight ahead, just as I did that day, and not give it another thought—until I thought about relaying this story to you. Although I had experienced something that *was* attractive to me, it held no power over me.

That's the way it is for me regarding any same-sex attractions that I still do have.

While I recognize those attractions when they occur, I'm able to keep walking straight ahead and not give them another thought. My attractions now are like that deflated beach ball at my feet on the sand at the bottom of the water, something which, as I said earlier, I can easily brush away or step around.

I believe that part of the reason I am able to do this is due to the transformative work that God has done in my life, but part of it is also due to the practical wisdom that God has given to me, through His Word and through the counsel of some other godly Christians.

The good news about this for those who are struggling with same-sex attractions, or any kinds of unwanted attractions, is that this same transformative power and collective wisdom is available to anyone who is willing to take hold of it and make use of it. I've seen others put these ideas into practice in their own lives just as effectively as I've been able to put them to use in my own, so I know they're transferrable.

Sometimes we need to truly "let it go," to let those fires die out, knowing that even if what we're feeling *might* be based on a valid need, God doesn't want us to satisfy that need in an invalid way. (And it reminds me of an old math joke which says, "Dear Algebra: Please stop asking us to find your x. She's never coming back. Don't ask y.")

By recognizing that I will simply never be able to satisfy certain desires, and by walking away from other desires, God has helped me to *cool* my desires for those things which I know can be harmful to me.

FUELING OUR DESIRES

On the flip side, God has also helped me to *fuel* my desires for those things which I know can be truly helpful to me.

When Lana was still alive, I found practical ways that I could deepen my love and affection for her beyond what it already was.

While the intimacy we shared at the beginning of our relationship was incredible, it grew even stronger as time passed. Why? In part, it was because I began to build up a database of experiences with her that was unparalleled.

Like many of the married men I know who have experienced same-sex attractions, my attractions to my wife were almost singular in their focus—meaning that I was hardly ever attracted to any woman other than her. While some people might point to this fact to say that I was never fully changed, from my point of view, this was a *huge* blessing to me.

The last thing I needed was to go from being predominantly attracted to men to being predominantly attracted to women! That wouldn't be a sign of healing. That would be a sign of sheer madness, just replacing one form of temptation with another. But what God did for me, and what He has done for others, was to put within me a singular attraction for my wife that was off the charts. And, I believe, this is the way it should be.

As the Bible says, "May your fountain be blessed, and may you rejoice in the wife of your youth. A loving doe, a graceful deer—may her breasts satisfy you always, may you ever be captivated by her love" (Proverbs 5:18-19).

Without being graphic, what I *can* say is that after building up hundreds of memories of intimate experiences with my wife over many weeks and months and years, I found that my desires would be stirred with barely a glimpse of her breasts near the neckline of her shirt. A fleeting look would cause me to smile for a *very* long time, stirring me in ways that a husband *should* be stirred toward his wife.

To experience something like this was always amazing to me, because in my pre-pubescent years, and even my early pubescent ones, I saw no difference between looking at a woman's breasts or looking at her elbows or her knees. They simply held no allure for me.

Yet, after being intimate with my wife again and again, and finally understanding in a deeper way that there was a built-in role that her breasts played in our intimacy, I began to see them differently. As the years went on, I was able to fully comprehend what the other guys in school were talking about, where they said that even a glimpse of a woman's breasts would provoke an immediate response within them.

As my database of experiences with my wife grew, it helped to fuel the fire in my heart that also helped to keep our romance alive.

Another step I took to focus my attention solely on my wife was to follow the advice of someone else who had walked this path before me.

As I share in my book, *What God Says About Sex*, a Christian friend encouraged me to give up the idea of ever pleasing myself sexually when I was alone, both before and after I got married. Rather than to ever enjoy the pleasure of sexual release by myself, this friend recommended that I only enjoy that experience when I was in the company of my wife.

This one piece of advice turned out to be one of the greatest blessings of our marriage, for even though I was tempted to do otherwise at times, it eventually became one of those *hluntheline* longings that C.S. Lewis describes in his book. My recognition that I simply wasn't going to fulfill my sexual desires in any way other than when I was with my wife took away any internal distress that such a stance could have caused.

As a result, my wife became my sole source of sexual pleasure in my life. The blessings from that one decision alone blissfully followed us for the rest of our marriage.

For instance, largely because of this decision, I never got into pornography, for there was no point in stirring those desires if I couldn't fulfill those desires. And because I never got into pornography, I never had to compare my wife to the myriad of other airbrushed models who appear in those images.

My wife's breasts truly satisfied me, first and foremost because I sincerely believe she was made uniquely by God Himself as a gift to me, but second, because I wasn't continually comparing her to anyone else. As my sole source of sexual delight, she became to me the most gorgeous person on the planet.

I'm not saying that others should do the exact same things which I had done to keep myself so singularly focused on my wife, although they turned out to be good pieces of advice for me, and they worked well in our situation.

What I *am* saying is that there *are* things we can all do to either cool our desires or fuel our desires. I know I was grateful to find some of these ways for myself—and I should add, on behalf of my wife, that *she* was very grateful, too!

LETTING GOD DEFINE US

I've also come to realize that my temptations don't define me. This was most apparent when I learned that the Bible says that Jesus was tempted in *every* way, just as we are, yet He was without sin.

In talking about Jesus, the writer of the book of Hebrews says, "For we do not have a High Priest who is unable to sympathize with our weaknesses, but we have one who has been tempted in every way, just as we are—yet was without sin. Let us then approach the throne of grace with confidence, so that we may receive mercy and find grace to help us in our time of need" (Hebrews 4:15-16).

If Jesus was tempted in *every* way, just as we are, then He was apparently tempted by homosexuality, too, as some of us obviously are. Yet no one who looks intently at the Scriptures would ever call Jesus gay any more than they would call Him a thief or a liar or an adulterer or a fornicator, because nothing in the Scriptures gives us any evidence that He was any of those things. Yet if Jesus really was tempted in every way, just as we are, then we can believe that He really was tempted toward all of these things as well.

But Jesus *wasn't defined* by His temptations—and neither are we. We're defined by the God who created us, the God who crafted us in our mothers' wombs.

When God made me, He made me a man, complete with all the male reproductive parts that declare me to be a man, including an X and Y chromosome in every cell of my body. (Women, on the other hand, and by scientific definition, have *two* X chromosomes in every cell of *their* bodies.)

I'm a man, through and through, created from conception to reproduce heterosexually, if God wanted me to reproduce. While I might have *feelings* toward men or be *tempted* to engage in sexual activities that go beyond heterosexuality, I'm not *defined* by those feelings. I'm not defined by my temptations.

I'm defined by the God who created me—and by the science which attests to the nature and the purposes for which I was created.

Does this mean it's wrong to want to have close male friends? Of course not! Does this mean it's wrong to be attracted to a man or be tempted to be with a man in a romantic or sexual way? Of course not!

Our desires for close friends, and our temptations toward things that might involve such close friends do not make us guilty of sin, just as Jesus wasn't guilty of sin for the desires and temptations that He faced. Again, as the writer of the book of Hebrews stated: "... we have one who has been tempted in every way, just as we are—yet was without sin."

As best as I can tell, our attractions and desires are formed by a combination of factors, some of which are related to nature (the way we were born), some to nurture (the way we were raised), and some to circumstances (the life experiences which we've had). This isn't rocket science, but rather a simple observation of human nature as expressed to me by hundreds of people who have shared their life experiences with me.

SHAPING OUR DESIRES

Our nature and our upbringing and our experiences really do serve to shape our "tastes" and our "desires," whether those tastes and desires are toward things that could end up being good for us or end up being harmful to us.

And our tastes and desires can be fueled or cooled in so many ways!

I'm amazed at the way smoking cigarettes was glamorized so much in my parents' generation, with ads touting the health benefits to people's lungs if they smoked. One ad famously proclaimed: "More doctors smoke Camels than any other cigarette."

Doctors actually advised patients to inhale cigarette smoke deeply and frequently in order to promote *healthier* lungs.

But now that smoking is scientifically linked to cancer, smoking has been demonized almost universally. Society as a whole has shifted its view dramatically on smoking, just like it has shifted its view on many other practices as well.

Believe it or not, when I was a child, I wore pajamas made with asbestos. Asbestos is an excellent flame retardant, so it was smart thinking to infuse the fabric of our clothes with it, especially the sleepwear of infants and children who might have trouble escaping from a burning bedroom.

But when people came to realize that those same asbestos fibers could make their way into people's lungs and cause lung cancer, society's thinking on the subject changed practically overnight.

In the same way, my view of same-sex attractions changed practically overnight as well, when God opened my eyes to the harmful effects of what I had done. While I can still see some of the positive aspects of engaging in a same-sex relationship, those benefits are extremely outweighed by the harm it could do to my life, not just from diseases like AIDS, which was killing many of the gay men my age in the 1980's, but because of the various other ways that homosexuality seemed to shortchange the fullness of the life which God had intended for me to live.

Because of this shift in my own thinking, I rarely let any fleeting thoughts regarding my same-sex attractions ever go much further than that—being just fleeting thoughts—just like I rarely (well, never) give a fleeting thought to the idea of buying a pair of asbestos pajamas for myself or for one of my kids.

This isn't to say that I couldn't, if I wanted to do so, *try* to blow some air back into that deflated beach ball. I could, I'm sure! But I don't *want* to because I *know* it would be like death to me if I did.

BLOWING UP OUR BEACHBALLS

Some of my friends, however, *have* tried to blow some air back into their beach balls, and I've seen them explode when they do.

For example, I have a friend who married one of the cutest girls I've ever known. Both he and his wife are extremely good-looking, and both are extremely personable.

My friend had wrestled with same-sex attractions prior to getting married, but after meeting this wonderful girl, they started dating and eventually got married in a picture-perfect wedding in a wooded wonderland.

I met up with my friend a year after his wedding, shocked to discover that he was getting a divorce. How could this be? He had been so in love with his girlfriend, and she had been so in love with him. Everything looked like it was going to work out so well.

But things hadn't worked out, he told me. I sat with him in a restaurant in his hometown for several hours, listening as he told me that he simply wasn't interested in her anymore physically. He wanted to go back to his gay lifestyle.

I was totally puzzled why this wasn't working out for him. I asked as many probing questions as I could, but couldn't find a reason.

It was only near the end of our conversation that he finally said to me, as if it were an off-hand comment, "Well, two weeks after we got married I *did* sleep with the man who catered our wedding." And somehow (surprisingly?), from there on out, his marriage began its downward spiral.

"I gave marriage a try," he said in conclusion, "and it didn't work out."

I wanted to scream: "You *didn't* give marriage a try! You didn't even give it *two weeks!*"

I was floored. And I was furious. My heart went out to his wife, a woman who would have been like a dream to most any other man, as she had been to him at one time, yet he had sabotaged his own marriage by his casual indiscretions, wrecking her life at the same time.

His failed marriage wasn't the result of his *suppression* of his same-sex desires; it was the result of his *indulgence* of those desires, fanning them into full flame, and burning many people along the way.

I have another friend who has never had a same-sex relationship in his life, but who had always wondered what it would be like to have one. He left his wonderings behind when he eventually got married to a woman he dearly loved, and they started a family together.

Years later, however, he confessed to me and to his wife that he was dangerously close to acting out on his homosexual feelings, saying that they had resurfaced after all these years.

He told me that he and his wife were hardly ever intimate anymore, due in part to some health issues she faced. Combining this with his lack of close male friends in the city where he lived, he said he was longing for intimacy and a closer connection with other men.

As we talked more about his same-sex attractions and why they had such a strong pull on him after all this time, he confessed to me that he was now viewing male porn on a daily basis. It was, for him, like reading the morning newspaper.

It was no surprise then, to him or to me, that he was now feeling dangerously close to acting out on his same-sex attractions.

Those feelings which he had been able to successfully keep at bay in the past were now threatening to overtake both him and his marriage, as he was feeding those feelings on a daily basis. Thankfully, my friend had the wisdom and the courage to call me when he was struggling, providing a relief valve of sorts so his temptations didn't consume him.

There's a folk tale about a father who told his son that there are two wolves that live within each of us, one of which wants to do right and one of which wants to do wrong. When asked by the son which wolf would win in the end, the father replied, "Whichever one you feed the most."

The Bible says there's a natural progression from *desiring* something that could be harmful us, to then *engaging* in it, to then *facing the consequences* for having engaged in it.

As the Apostle James says, "When tempted, no one should say, 'God is tempting me.' For God cannot be tempted by evil, nor does He tempt anyone; but each one is tempted when, by his own evil desire, he is dragged away and enticed. Then, after desire has conceived, it gives birth to sin; and sin, when it is full- grown, gives birth to death" (James 1:13-15).

This is the natural progression of our harmful desires. Thankfully, there's an exit ramp from this harmful cycle—and God wants us to take it every time. It's not always easy, but God says in His Word that He will *always* provide a way out, which I'll share more about in the next chapter (see 1 Corinthians 10:13).

DECLARING OUR VICTORY

I want to give you one more practical suggestion to help you and those you love find freedom from your struggles.

I was taking a walk with a friend one day through a state park here in Illinois when we came upon a sign telling us that a certain battle had taken place on that spot during America's war for independence.

When I looked closer at the plaque, it said that this battle had taken place sometime in the year 1779.

"1779?" I said aloud to my friend. "Didn't we win our independence in 1776? Why were they still fighting a battle here in 1779?"

Then I remembered. Of course! July 4th, 1776, was the day we *declared* our independence. It still took more than seven years of bloody battles until the war for our freedom was finally over.

Just because we *declared* our independence in 1776 didn't mean that our battles *ended* on that date.

In fact, in many ways, the day of our declaration was the day the battles really began in earnest. And those battles didn't end until more than seven years later, when the U.S. and England finally signed the *Treaty of Versailles* on September 3rd, 1783.

I don't know of anyone, however, who celebrates the signing of the *Treaty of Versailles*, let alone remembers the date when the signing took place and the war officially ended.

What people celebrate, and what we remember the most, is the day we *declared* our freedom, the date which has been indelibly etched into every American's mind—July 4th, 1776.

I feel the same way about the day I decided to put my faith in Christ for everything in my life—February 9, 1987.

That date has been indelibly etched into my mind as well, because it was on that date that I put my faith in Christ for everything in my life, declaring my freedom from the grip that homosexuality once held over my life up until that point.

That's not to say that there haven't been some skirmishes since then, or that there haven't been some times when those temptations have tried to rise up within me. That's no surprise! That's the way life is! That's the way temptation works!

But to say that someone hasn't been set free from something which once held them captive, just because they occasionally still have battles to fight, is like saying that the United States wasn't free on the day they declared their freedom, but only at some later date after all their battles were finally put to rest—a date which hardly anyone even remembers anymore.

Anyone who has ever had to give up something they've enjoyed—even if it's something that they've *known* will be ultimately destructive to them—knows that *making the decision* to give up that thing is just as important as *winning the battles* that follow such a decision.

Life's too short to continue living in something which you know will be ultimately destructive to you.

I want to encourage you to put your faith in Christ for everything in your life, and I want to encourage your family and friends to do the same.

Declare your freedom *today* from whatever is tempting you, and take hold of the freedom that God is offering to you through His Son, Jesus Christ.

Then *you'll* be able to sing, like the *psalmist* sang, and like *I've* been able to sing, "I run in the path of Your commands, for You have set my heart free" (Psalm 119:32).

Study Guides For Chapters 7 & 8

STUDY GUIDE FOR CHAPTER 7: "THE VALUE OF A LOVING CHURCH"

Chapter Summary

Some people think the church has responded abysmally to the topic of homosexuality. But the author says his experience has been just the opposite. He says:

- he has found the church to be a sanctuary, a refuge, and a place of healing and acceptance,
- and it is "out there," out in "the world," that he has felt vilified, mistreated, disrespected, threatened, bullied, shamed, and demeaned.

He asks people who feel the church has given a poor response on this topic to share what their personal experiences have been—not telling second-hand stories they've heard about a few un-Christlike churches which are featured regularly in the news.

He believes:

- the church is the hope of the world,
- Christ is still perfecting the church to become His bride,
- and the leaders and people in the various churches where he's attended have been among the most caring, helpful, and kind people in regards to this issue, even back when he was still involved in homosexuality.

The author acknowledges that his experiences may not be representative of everyone else's, and he has apologized on behalf of the church to those who have felt otherwise. But from his perspective, the church as a whole has had an amazing record on how they've dealt with this topic.

He concludes by saying that the historical church, as documented in the Bible, has been helpful to him regarding this topic:

- because he sees that people in the church in Corinth were set free from homosexuality within 20-22 years after Christ walked the earth,

- because he sees that this is not a 21st century issue, but one that God has been addressing as far back as 2,000 years ago, 3,300 years ago, and 4,000 years ago,
- and because he sees that God's warnings on this issue are as clear and as strong as they could possibly be.

The author asks readers who feel the Bible is not clear or not strong on this topic to think how they would have *wanted* God to word His warnings in order to make them any clearer or stronger than they already are.

He then notes that the reason God is so clear and strong on this topic is not because God is repulsed by homosexuality, but because, having created our sexuality, God knows how powerful, yet how dangerous, sex can be if used in ways it was not designed to be used.

QUESTIONS FOR REFLECTION & DISCUSSION

Read Revelation 19:7-9. Why do you think Jesus still loves the church today and looks forward to the great wedding supper of the Lamb? What encouragement can Jesus' love for the church give you about your own view of the church?

Read Leviticus 18:22, Leviticus 20:13, Romans 1:24-32, and 1 Corinthians 6:9-12. Can you think of any words of warning God might have used which would have been stronger or clearer than those already recorded in the Bible? What wording would *you* use if you were to warn people about something they were tempted to do but could harm them? Would your wording have been stronger or weaker than the words that are already recorded in the Bible?

Read Romans 5:8. Why do we as Christians *not* call for the death penalty for those who engage in homosexual acts? What has changed since the coming of Christ? The penalty? Or the fact that the penalty has already been paid?

What has been your personal experience with the church on this topic? Have you heard leaders in your church speak about this issue in ways that have been mean-spirited, hateful, and demeaning to gays? Or has your experience been the opposite, that leaders in your church speak compassionately, lovingly, and helpfully to those dealing with same-sex attractions?

Why do you think the same few churches continue to grab headlines whenever they speak in horrific ways about gays? Do you believe those few churches speak for the church as a whole? Do they speak for you?

What does the author suggest people do who *are* part of churches where gays are denounced, demeaned, and humiliated? Would someone have to go to a gay-affirming church to find a different approach? Or do you think there are churches which believe homosexual acts are sins, yet are still able to treat people who are experiencing same-sex attractions with dignity and respect?

What significance do you find in the fact that the Bible says that the people in the church in Corinth had once been involved in homosexuality, yet adds, "and that is what some of you *were*"? What hope can these words give to those who are experiencing same-sex attractions, but who do not want to act on them?

What does it say about God's awareness of this issue, and heart regarding this issue, that He would have made such strong and clear warnings some 2,000 years ago in the days of Jesus, some 3,300 years ago in the days of Moses, and some 4,000 years ago in the days of Abraham? Do you think His warnings indicate His shock that anyone would consider acting on their same-sex attractions or because He knew quite well that people would be tempted to do this?

STUDY GUIDE FOR CHAPTER 8: "A FEW WORDS ABOUT TEMPTATION"

CHAPTER SUMMARY

Temptations come to everyone, just as they came to Jesus. But our temptations:

- don't define us, just as they didn't define Jesus,
- don't control us, just as they didn't control Jesus,
- and don't have to overwhelm us, as God says He will always provide a way of escape from our temptations—and He wants us to take those ways of escape every time.

The author suggests several practical ideas to help cool unhealthy desires and fuel healthy desires, including:

- recognizing that some activities simply cannot and should not ever take place, thereby reducing their tug on our hearts,
- never trying to breathe air back into those deflated beach balls at our feet by calling someone "just to keep in touch," or letting thoughts or gazes linger on that which is unhealthy,
- and committing to enjoying sexual fulfillment only when in the company of our spouse, including self pleasure.

He also says we should not be surprised that temptations continue even after we have declared our intent to walk away from them, just as the battles of the American Revolution continued for several years after the *Declaration of Independence* was signed. Declaring our freedom is just as important as fighting the battles which follow. We shouldn't be surprised, however, that battles may follow, even for years to come, just as the battles of the American Revolution continued until the signing of the *Treaty of Versailles*, more than seven years after the signing of the *Declaration of Independence*.

QUESTIONS FOR REFLECTION & DISCUSSION

Read 2 Corinthians 5:17. How does this verse relate to the author's statement: "When God transformed my life, He didn't just change me from a caterpillar into a better caterpillar. He changed me into a whole new creation"?

Read John 10:10. How does this verse relate to the author's story about the man who ended up in a church that was dry, dull, and boring, saying, "I gave up drugs for THIS?" Have you ever felt there was *more* to the Christian life than what you were experiencing? Do you feel you've found the abundant life which Jesus says is available to those who have put their faith in Him—or are you still looking for it?

Read Proverbs 4:23 and Proverbs 5:18-19. Why did King Solomon to say to guard our hearts? What can happen if we let down our guard? How can we guard our hearts and refocus our attention on that which God wants us to desire?

Read Hebrews 4:15-16. What do these verses say about Jesus' temptations and whether or not those temptations were considered sin? Why wasn't Jesus defined by His temptations? Why shouldn't we define ourselves by ours?

Read 1 Corinthians 10:13. What does God say He will provide for us every time we're tempted? What are some ways the author says people can cool or fuel their desires?

Why might some people be surprised that someone who has declared their freedom in this area might still face some temptations? Considering the fact that most Americans celebrate July 4th, 1776, as a national holiday rather than September 3rd, 1783, what does this say about the reality of facing ongoing battles in gaining our ultimate freedom? What does this say about the importance of declaring our freedom, relative to finally winning that freedom?

Chapter 9:

A Few Words About Pain

In which I share how pain can tempt us to do things which we might never have considered doing otherwise—and how you can help others through their own painful times.

When we're in pain, we can sometimes be tempted to do things we might never have considered doing otherwise.

Even Jesus was tempted from time to time to walk away from His Father's will, right up to the night before He died. Jesus pleaded in prayer for any other way than the way that stood before Him.

In the end, however, Jesus yielded to His Father's will, saying, "…yet not My will, but Yours be done" (Luke 22:42b).

Temptation is real, and I'm not beyond temptation, either. Lest you think I don't really understand the ongoing struggle that many people face daily, I'd like to share with you how temptation has still played a role in my life, especially during a time of very deep pain.

Soon after my wife Lana was diagnosed with cancer, the doctors told us that it had unfortunately already spread throughout her entire body. There was nothing they could do to stop its rapid growth.

The day we got the news, I cried in my room for 24 hours straight. I couldn't come out, even to eat. My mom had died of the same type of cancer, and I couldn't imagine watching my wife go through it as well. I knew I was facing some of the darkest days I would ever face in my life.

During the months that followed, the pain I felt at the thought of losing Lana was becoming unbearable. One day, she asked if we could talk about something that was bothering her. She said she was getting jealous just thinking about whoever I might marry next in the event that she died.

This was a conversation I *did not* want to have. I couldn't imagine losing her, let alone living my life without her, let alone trying to imagine having another relationship with anyone else but her!

I couldn't see how anyone else could ever understand me like she had understood me or forgive me like she had forgiven me or have an off-the-charts sex life with me as she had had with me. The list of my objections in my mind went on and on.

But a few days later, in the midst of my grief and the pain of thinking about it all, a new thought came into my head—a thought that I didn't like even more. While I couldn't picture ever being intimate with any other woman for the rest of my life, the thought that came to me was this: "But if the right *man* comes along... (or the *wrong* man, as the case might be)."

"What?!?!" I thought, as the insides of my brain began to explode.

"Yes," I told myself, "I know what God's Word says. And, yes, I've spoken on this for a lot of years and I've seen God do some amazing things. But I'm tired. I'm hurting. And I'm in pain. I vaguely remember something from long ago that gave me some kind of relief from pain before."

I couldn't believe it. I hadn't given serious consideration to homosexuality for nearly three decades. The thought of it all scared me so much that I told Lana the next day what had happened and why. She was my best prayer partner in life, even for things like this.

I asked her to pray for me, as she had done whenever I confessed anything to her in the past, on any topic that had been bothering me. Lana prayed with me, and within two weeks, God answered those prayers.

During those two weeks, I felt as if a dark cloud were hovering over me that entire time, something like a fog or a weight. I couldn't pinpoint where it was coming from or how to get rid of it. All I could do was to trust that God would walk me through it.

GOD'S ANSWER

After two weeks of wrestling with why I would even *think* about something like this, God spoke to me—very clearly—three times on the same day.

The first time God spoke to me was soon after I woke up. It was a Sunday morning, and I sat down to have some quiet time before church.

As I opened my Bible, I happened to be reading Chapter 1 in the book of Romans, the very same passage I had read when the light first dawned on me all those years ago when God wanted to deal with my same-sex attractions. As I read Paul's words once again, it all came back to me.

"That's right," I thought. "That's why I would never go back into homosexuality. I know it would be like death to me if I did."

Later that same morning, as I was sitting in church, our pastor said something in passing about the topic of homosexuality. What he said was perhaps the simplest and most profound statement I had ever heard on the subject in all my years of looking into it, reading up on it, and talking to others about it.

My pastor said, "If you do something that God says not to do, it won't go well for you."

When he said those words, it was like a second and brighter light in a three-way light bulb turned on, lighting my mind even brighter.

I thought, "Yes, Lord, That's right. That's why I don't do it, too."

Later that night, God spoke to me a third time—this time through a friend. I was talking to him about my fears of losing Lana, and how the thought of homosexuality had come back to my mind.

He told me the same thing had happened to him when he faced the possibility of losing his wife a few years earlier. He said he had wondered at the time if maybe it was God's way of telling him that it would be okay now if he did want to go into homosexuality.

"Of course not!" I said. "That's not what God would want you to do, and that's not what God would want me to do to ease the pain that I'm feeling now, either!"

It was one thing for me to consider such a thought in my own mind, but quite another to hear such similar words coming out of the mouth of my friend!

As soon as he spoke those words, it was like the full brightness of that three-way bulb had turned on inside my head.

"Of course not!" I thought again. "Although my pain is definitely real, I *know* that's not the way God wants me to deal with my pain!"

My goal in all the years that I've ministered to people who are struggling with their same-sex attractions has been to help *relieve* their pain, not increase it. And while I know I can't help relieve people of *all their pain*, my hope is that I can help to at least keep them from the *wrong kind of pain*—the pain they might inflict on themselves by doing whatever they want to do, instead of doing whatever God wants them to do.

Just like we may not have a choice regarding the kinds of temptations we face, we also don't always have a choice regarding what kinds of curve balls life throws at us, either.

We do however, have a choice about how we will respond to those curve balls.

THE DARKNESS LIFTS

In that moment, with the flip of that third light switch, I felt as if the darkness that had been hanging over my head for the previous two weeks lifted completely.

God had spoken to me clearly three times that day: first from the Word of God, second from the pastor at my church, and third from the words of a Christian friend who had been through a similar struggle. And each time, God helped me to realize that there was no pain on earth that was worth throwing myself into an even deeper pain.

My head was instantly clear again, and it's stayed clear ever since, now five years later. Although my pain and heartache over possibly losing Lana, and then actually losing her, continued throughout her final days and on into the weeks and months that followed her death, I was able to avoid that pain the I *did* have control over.

That night, after God had spoken so clearly to me three times, I was able to tell Lana that her prayers for me had been answered. I was able to tell her that she would never have to worry about me going back into homosexuality again, even if she were to die, for God had broken through that fog once again.

As a footnote, Lana gave me a beautiful gift one day, a few months later, when she brought up the topic of remarriage again. She said she had been thinking more about it, and she wanted to give me her blessing in hopes I *would* get married again someday. She said that she was so blessed to have me as her husband that she knew I would be a blessing to someone else in the future.

Although I still didn't want to talk about the idea any more that day than I did a few months earlier, I was so thankful she was able to have peace in her heart regarding my future, and that she had given me her blessing if there ever were to come a time when I actually thought about getting married again.

After this incident, I talked to another pastor friend about what I had experienced, and he gave me a helpful perspective. He said that my thoughts weren't surprising, as when we're in pain, we're often tempted to turn to anything that might possibly give us some relief from that pain, many times being drawn to something in our past. King Solomon said as much in Proverbs 26:11. (I'll let you look that one up yourself.)

I tell you that story to let you know that it's not surprising to me, either, if you or someone you know still struggles with same-sex attractions from time to time, even after many years of living in freedom—and especially when deep pain is involved.

None of us get out of this world without temptations, not even Jesus.

It's understandable that some pain seems so unbearable that the idea of giving into temptation seems like no big deal anymore.

It's also understandable if you, as a loving and compassionate follower of Jesus Christ, might feel like telling those you love to go ahead and give in to their temptations. You might feel like telling them that it probably won't be as bad for them as whatever they're facing now. You might feel like telling them to go ahead and enjoy whatever relief they can find from their pain, at least for a little while.

Can I encourage you, though, to stand strong? Can I encourage you to be wise as your loved ones go through this, offering them *true* wisdom to *truly* help them through whatever they're going through?

As my pastor reminded me, "If you do something that God says not to do, it won't go well for you."

You might think that the pain your friends or family members are facing now is unbearable, but I can assure you that their pain will be far worse if they give in to their temptations—especially if God has said *not* to do what they're wanting to do. It simply won't go well for them. It just won't.

I can't tell you all the things that could possibly go wrong, because I can't foresee all of those things. But I know, in this case especially, that Father really does know best.

If you do something that God says not to do, it won't go well for you. And it won't go well for those you love, either.

A CONSOLATION PRIZE?

Some people sincerely believe that being gay is the first-best option that God has in mind for their lives or the lives of those they love. They believe that God *must* have made them that way because they can't think of any other reason for why they feel the way they feel.

Other people think that while being gay might not be the *first-best* option, it is, perhaps, at least a close *second*, a consolation prize for those who didn't get whatever it takes to get the first-best option in their lives. While they might believe that being gay is not ideal, it's probably as good as it's ever going to get here on earth for themselves or for those they love.

But God says that homosexuality is neither the first-best option *nor* a second-best option. God says it's actually *a harmful and destructive option*, not only for those who engage in it, but also for His plans and purposes for sexuality and His plans and purposes for the world as He has created it.

Some people will say, "But what harm does homosexuality really do? Why not just let people do whatever they want? They're not hurting anyone."

I've already shared a few of the harms that *I've* faced because of *my* homosexuality: the very real possibility of contracting AIDS and losing my life; the very real possibility of shortchanging myself and my wife from what eventually became the most off-the-charts relationship we've ever had in our lives; and the very real possibility of shortchanging God from the plans and purposes for which He gave us the gift of sex in the first place, to create intimacy between my wife and I, and to create children who both my wife and I and God could love.

People might object and say there are ways around each of those harms. Yes, there are. But I've barely gotten started and I've already listed three *major* harms that could have come upon me had I stayed on the path of homosexuality. The list of harms goes on and on.

I doubt that those who say that homosexuality doesn't hurt anyone has ever sat with a wife who's in a mess of tears because her husband has just left her for another man, telling her that he was gay, has always been gay, and that this will be the best thing for everyone involved.

I doubt that those who say this have ever sat with the children of someone who has abandoned them to go pursue their own desires rather than fathering or mothering the children they've already sired.

I doubt they've ever sat with a broken-hearted girlfriend who's afraid she'll never get married now because the man of her dreams has just told her he thinks he's gay and might never overcome it—so he's gone ahead and slept with another man just to see if it's true.

From my vantage point, I've seen homosexuality do a *lot* of harm. And yes, I've seen heterosexuality do a lot of harm, too. That's because sex is like electricity: extremely powerful and useful when contained within its proper restraints, but equally powerful and destructive when unleashed beyond those restraints.

I hurt for those who have been deceived into thinking that there's no way out for them from the temptations they're facing, so they give in to their temptations instead. I hurt for them, especially, because I *know* there's another way.

I also hurt for those who are left behind as those with same-sex attractions give in to their temptations, leaving a trail of destruction in their wake.

Someone might say, "Well, it's better for someone with those attractions to walk away now than to stay in an unhealthy marriage and cause more pain in the future."

I *would* agree, if causing more pain in the future were the only option.

But such thinking discounts the fact that God is still in the life-changing business. It discounts the fact that God has helped, and continues to help, people overcome all kinds of struggles and all kinds temptations in their lives, just like He's helped me and so many people I know.

Such thinking also discounts the fact that marriages face all kinds of problems, and some people use *this* as an excuse to not deal with the other very real problems in their marriages.

TRADING ONE PAIN FOR ANOTHER

Although God has spoken clearly and strongly on this issue in the Bible and in our hearts, pain has a way of decreasing our ability to hear from God—unless we allow that pain to drive us closer to Him.

I've seen many times how pain and temptation have affected not only myself, but also those I love.

I have a friend whose father committed adultery. When the truth came out, my friend's mother was so grieved that she tumbled into despair. My friend and his siblings followed suit.

Because my friend's relationship with his father had already been fractured prior to this, the pain of his father's adultery and his mother's despair made him even more susceptible to his same-sex temptations. My friend eventually succumbed to the advances of a much older man—older than his own father.

This older man's affirmation and affection met a valid need in my friend's life, helping fill the gaping holes in his heart. To me, however, it seemed ironic that the pain that resulted from *one* invalid sexual act caused my friend to turn to *another* invalid sexual act in order to relieve that pain. My friend hated his father because of his adultery, yet my friend went on to commit adultery with this older man, as the older man was also married to a woman and had a family.

The older man's family then fell apart when *his* adultery was discovered! Here my friend was trying to deal with the pain of his father's adultery, yet in trying to deal with it, he committed adultery just like his father had done, except with a man.

I'm not sure if my friend ever made the connection between what his father had done to his family and what my friend himself had done to this other man's family.

I'm sure my friend, and my friend's father, and even this older man were all trying to meet their valid needs, but they were trying to meet them in ways which were *massively* invalid, leaving a trail of destruction for years to come. Each of the parties involved simply traded one pain for another.

I have another friend who was a leader in the ex-gay movement for many years. He had personally helped me in several significant ways at the beginning of my own journey.

In recent years, however, I've learned that he's gone back into homosexuality—leaving behind a second wife and family in the process. He left his first wife before he was a Christian to go into homosexuality initially.

While this friend had done so much to help me and others, his second marriage proved to be extremely difficult for a variety of reasons, not simply because of his same-sex attractions.

When my friend found a man who captured his attention, he decided to go back into homosexuality. His new love interest convinced him that he must have been reading the Scriptures wrong all this time.

If I didn't understand the connection between pain and temptation so well, I might have been puzzled as to how he could have suddenly come to this "new" interpretation of the Scriptures which led him to believe that homosexuality was now okay, but that honoring his life-long commitment to his wife and family was no longer necessary.

It's one thing to think it's okay to be gay, but it's another thing to use that belief as a justification to abandon the other parts of Scripture that you already know to be true. (Or as Mark Twain is famously quoted as saying: "It's not the parts of the Bible that I don't understand that bother me; it's the parts of the Bible that I do understand.")

While my friend says he feels freer now than ever before, and I'm sure he does, I can imagine his wife and family will sadly feel the sting of his decision for years to come.

I'm not casting stones at my friend. I've already confessed to you that I know what it's like to be in such pain that we can be tempted to chuck everything we've ever learned or taught or believed or heard or read in God's Word in order to find relief. I get it. I really do.

But it also saddens my heart every time I hear something like this happen because, with the right wisdom from God, the support of a strong local church, and the touch of a few loving friends, so much of this tragic pain could be avoided.

NOT EVERYONE HAS A LANA

Some people might think I was able to handle my same-sex attractions better than others because of my family upbringing being so positive or because I had someone like Lana by my side. I'm sure people who say this have a point. I *do* believe those things have helped me tremendously, and I'm extremely grateful for them.

I remember telling my story to someone one day, about how I had left homosexuality behind and gone on to marry Lana, the woman of my dreams. This person knew Lana as well and said, "Yes, but not everyone has a Lana."

I was silenced by her statement for a few days, thinking through what she had said and letting the truth of her words sink in.

My friend was right. Not everyone *does* have a Lana, and for that I'm truly sorry. But after a few more days of contemplation, I realized another truth: I didn't have a Lana anymore, either!

How was *I* making it, and going to continue making it, without this incredible life-partner by my side? Well, I'm making it because I'm going to keep doing what God has shown me to do, with or without a Lana by my side. You see, it's not about having a Lana, or not having a Lana (as much as I wish everyone could have one of those!)

It's about finding God's "way out" from the dark clouds of temptation when they come—a way out which God says He will *always* provide. As the Bible says: "No temptation has seized you except what is common to man. And God is faithful; He will not let you be tempted beyond what you can bear. But when you are tempted, He will also provide a way out so that you can stand up under it" (1 Corinthians 10:13).

Lana helped me, for sure, but God has provided other "ways out" as well.

Even in the darkest hours of my life, God has provided a way out for me through His Word, through His Church, and through some strong Christian friends, including Lana.

When I couldn't find a way out on my own, God answered our prayers to help me find one.

God can use *all kinds of things* to provide a way of escape for us, but these three are especially helpful: staying in His Word, staying in His Church, and staying in fellowship with strong Christian friends.

YOU CAN HELP!

This is where *you* come in! *You* can be the friend that your loved ones need when they're going through times of pain and suffering.

You can be their true "pain reliever," not by telling them to "go for" something which could possibly provide some short-term relief, but in the long term would eventually cause more pain than ever before.

You can come alongside those you love to walk with them during their times of greatest need.

One of the greatest tragedies I hear these days is when long-time, seemingly-strong Christians don't feel they have a friend or a family member in whom they can truly confide.

A famous Christian singer came out as gay recently, shocking his wife, his fans, and his friends. None of those people closest to him had any idea he had been wrestling with same-sex attractions for years.

The saddest part of his story to me was that he felt he had no one with whom he could share his struggles. Not that those around him wouldn't have been *glad* to help him if he did open up, but for whatever reason, he felt like he couldn't be honest with them.

By the time he finally did confess his same-sex attractions to his wife and his family and his friends, he was already fully committed to leaving his family behind and going full throttle into homosexuality. There was no stopping him at that point, and the splash he made when he landed in the waters of homosexuality are still making waves today.

In an interview after coming out, this singer said he felt so relieved from all the pain he had kept hidden inside for years, adding, "I don't believe God hates me anymore."

While I'm glad he knows now that God doesn't hate him, the truth is that God *never did* hate him. God loved him even while he was still struggling in secret with his same-sex attractions.

Somehow he had believed a lie that because of his attractions, God must have hated him, when the truth was that God had loved him all along, same-sex attractions or not.

This singer had exchanged the truth of God for a lie, and that lie led him to leave his wife and family behind, thinking he was doing them a favor. Having kept his struggle in the dark for so long, it never had a chance to benefit from the light.

My encouragement to you is to help those you love open up about the pain they're feeling. Give them permission to talk about what's really going on in their hearts and minds. Offer a listening ear if they ever want to talk, then, as you have the opportunity, speak the truth into their lives, in love, wherever you notice that lies have taken over.

If it sounds like I'm sounding an alarm, trying to warn people from pursuing homosexuality, that's because I am! I'm trying to warn them just like God tried to warn me—and eventually succeeded!

God gives us His warnings because of His great love for us, not because of His great hatred for us. And God wants us to warn others from a place of love as well.

THE TROUBLE WITH TROUBLE

As I close out this chapter, I'd like to share one more story about pain with you, and how pain can drive people to do what they might never have done otherwise.

This story, however, is about a fictional character in a book, a man who was outed as gay several years after the book series in which he appeared had been published.

In these books, the man was featured as a hero and described by the author, and many of the books' readers, as "the epitome of goodness."

Several years after the books were published, the author responded to a question about the books, and in her response, the author delicately made a statement about this character, saying, "I always thought of him as gay."

Readers were rocked by this statement in various ways: some readers rejoiced that one of their most beloved characters in all of literature was gay, while other readers were totally caught off guard, trying to see how one of their favorite characters could have ever possibly been gay. The way this character is now perceived has been forever altered by that author's seven-word sound bite.

I was one of those readers who was totally caught off guard. But as I thought more about the author's statement, and as I considered some of the passages in the books which described his life story, I could see how he certainly *could* have been gay, especially in light of what he said about his formative years.

Looking back at his story again, this character described the time in his life when he was supposedly gay like this: "Two months of insanity, of cruel dreams, and neglect of the only two members of my family left to me.... He ran while I was left to bury my sister and learn to live with my guilt, and my terrible grief, the price of my shame."

Even though this comes from a work of fiction, I've seen it happen often enough in reality to know that his words describe, in a powerful way, how pain can drive any of us to do things we might never have considered doing otherwise. Had this character had a friend like you, his story may have turned out differently. :)

There's a reason why people in pain try to run to anything that might possibly relieve it. "The trouble with trouble," I've heard it said, "is that it usually starts out as a whole lot of fun."

But don't let pain drive you or your friends or your family members into something which would cause even deeper pain in the end— especially when there's a better way.

God *wants* to help us relieve our pain, when the time is right, and He *wants* to fulfill our valid needs, but in valid ways.

I pray you'll encourage your friends to do the same. You might just save them from a whole lot more pain.

As the Bible says: "My brothers, if one of you should wander from the truth and someone should bring him back, remember this: Whoever turns a sinner from the error of his way will save him from death and cover over a multitude of sins" (James 5:19-20).

Chapter 10:

The Importance Of Free Will

———— ◈ ————

In which I share about the importance of letting others exercise their own free will— just as God lets you exercise yours.

———— ◈ ————

The majority of people with whom I've spoken regarding their same-sex attractions are people who have sought me out. They've either heard me speak, read my testimony, or heard my story from a friend or family member.

The beauty of this is that the majority of people with whom I've spoken have *wanted* to hear what I have to say. They've been intrigued by the idea that they might not have to keep living in something that they've neither asked for nor desired.

This is perhaps one of the reasons why most of the people I've talked to have found my take on this subject to be one of *great hope*, as they're often wanting to experience the same freedom for themselves that they've seen in my life.

But I would also like to tell you some stories about a few of the people whom *I* have sought out to talk to about this issue.

Some of these people have been men with whom I've had a relationship in the past, and I've wanted to share with them what God has done for me.

Some have been friends who were in the lifestyle back when I was in it, but with whom I had not been intimately involved.

Some have been people I've simply met throughout my life for whom I've felt nudged to share my story.

I'm glad to say that I've almost always found a receptive audience in such people, at least for an initial hearing. I don't push it, but I also don't hold back if they're willing to listen, which they often are. My friends have listened to me tell my story, and I've listened to their heartfelt thoughts in return. I've always appreciated these opportunities to share.

But I think it's also important to let you know that the end results of many of these conversations have not caused *any* outward change in these people's lives, at least not that I've been able to see.

As of this writing, not one of my former partners have come to the same conclusions to which I have come. Not one of my gay friends from my former days in homosexuality have had the same life-changing experience that I have had, even after hearing my story in depth and spending time together in prayer afterward. I was only partly joking earlier in the book when I said that it only takes one psychologist to change a lightbulb, "but the lightbulb has to really *want* to change."

Still, I feel good about the fact that I've been able to talk to each of these men and share my story with them. And, on several occasions, I've felt that it was not just *me* wanting to share my story with them, but *God Himself* who had set up our meetings.

By telling you these stories, I want to *encourage* you to keep sharing with those around you, regardless of whether or not you ever see the results of your sharing. I also want to encourage you to share in a way that honors and respects the decisions your friends and family members have made and which, in the end, maintains your loving friendships with them.

As the Bible says, "If I have the gift of prophecy and can fathom all mysteries and all knowledge, and if I have a faith that can move mountains, but have not love, I am nothing" (1 Corinthians 13:2).

A DIVINE ENCOUNTER

On one occasion, I took a personal trip across the country to visit a friend and take him to a large men's conference (the conference was large, not the men).

Prior to that weekend, I really felt God was prompting me to be willing to share my testimony with my friend. He had never struggled with homosexuality, but I still felt, for the sake of our ongoing friendship, it was important to share this significant piece of my life with him.

And I really thought this was the weekend to do it. Although I was nervous and hesitant, I was willing. I tried to bring up the topic two or three times while we were together, but every time our conversation shifted before I could share.

When the time finally came for me to fly back home, I boarded the plane, feeling a bit down because I wasn't able to share with him what I felt God had been putting on my heart to share.

As I sat in my seat on the plane home, wondering how I could have misheard God so badly, a man sat down in the seat next to me and opened up a huge, hardback study Bible, laying it out on his tray table in front of him. It was the exact same study Bible that I had first bought when I had become a Christian so many years earlier. Mine was now worn and tattered, while his was still fresh and brand-spanking new.

He had opened it up to the first page of the first book of the New Testament, the book of Matthew.

I looked up to see who was sitting down next to me, and, to my amazement, it was a friend from our college days together some 15 years earlier!

We both knew each other as gay back then, and we had even talked about having an intimate encounter together one night. But moments before we did, something stopped me in my tracks.

I deferred, telling him that I didn't feel right about it for some reason. I never knew why, and I never did enter into a sexual relationship with him. We continued to be friends, though, and ran into each other from time to time during our days on campus.

As I sat next to him now on that plane, I reached back into the recesses of my brain to try to pull out his name. When it finally came to me, I blurted it out.

He looked at me, blurted out my name, too, and I don't know which of us was more surprised that we were there, "randomly" sitting next to each other on that plane!

I asked him about the Bible he had opened up on the tray table in front of him.

He told me that his mom had given it to him just before he had gotten on the plane, telling him that she thought he should read it. She had been praying for him for years, hoping to help him get his life in order. He told me he didn't even know where to start, as he had never before read the Bible for himself. That's why he opened it up to the first book of the New Testament, because he saw that's where the stories about Jesus were.

I told him that was a *great* place to start, that I had the exact same Bible, and that the words of Jesus in the book of Matthew had actually changed my life forever, leading me out of homosexuality for good. (It was the story of the blind men in Matthew, Chapter 9, where Jesus asked them, "Do you believe that I am able to do this?")

After my disappointing weekend of feeling blocked at every turn from sharing my testimony with my other friend, I was astounded that here on my return trip, *this* door had opened, and opened up wide, with a table set for the two of us by God Himself!

My friend was astounded as well and was eager to hear whatever I had to say, and, if I listened closely enough, I could have probably heard his mother shouting a few "Amens" and "Hallelujahs" of her own off in the distance somewhere, knowing that God would indeed answer her prayers as soon as her son opened up that Special Book.

Little could his mother have known that God was going to provide a *Living Testament* to sit right next to her son at the same time, one who could confirm and give testimony to what he was about to read in the New Testament.

I shared my story with him, just like I've shared it with you in this book.

My friend was fully engaged during the entire flight, asking questions, telling stories, and relating both the joys and frustrations of being a gay man in the city in which he lived.

We finished our time together with a prayer and a hug, each going our separate ways, and each shaking our heads at the Divine Encounter that God had just set up for us.

Here I had been feeling so strongly to share my story that weekend, but it turned out *not* to be with my friend who came to the men's conference with me and who had never struggled with this issue. It turned out to be with a friend from a lifetime ago who was very open to my message and very actively involved in homosexuality right up to that day.

TRUSTING GOD

I wish I could tell you that my friend's life changed dramatically in the days that followed, and that he has chosen to follow Christ just like I had chosen to follow Christ. But as far as I know, that didn't happen that day, and it still hasn't happened to this day.

I can't help but think, however, that God had *something* in mind for my sharing that day—because He did something that I could have never orchestrated in the same way on my own. And, as I said earlier, it took *years* for me to change my thinking on this topic until that one day when everything I had heard up to that point finally clicked.

I have to trust that the same God who set up that Divine Encounter on the plane will use it somehow to draw my friend closer to Himself as much as possible.

I also know that God gives people free will, the freedom to make their own decisions about whatever they're going to do with their lives and the paths they're going to follow. As Bruce says to God in the movie *Bruce Almighty*:

"How do you make somebody love you without affecting their free will?"

"Welcome to My world, son," God replies. "You come up with the answer for that, and we'll talk."

Free will is one of the most beautiful, yet one of the most difficult things we can offer to anyone. But God offers it to each of us so freely, and I believe He wants us to offer it to others—even when it's so hard to do.

TRUE FRIENDS

I've taken several other trips, some for business and some for pleasure, to several other cities around the world where I've been able to talk to some of my former gay friends.

In each of those meetings, we've been able to renew our friendships, be mutually encouraged by our time together, and I've been able to share my story with them as I shared it with my college friend on the plane that day.

Sometimes my friends and I have been able to stay in touch afterward by phone or email or social media. But having shared my testimony with them, and having listened to their stories in return, I've generally not brought up the topic again. I've left the conversations in their courts, continuing to keep alive our genuine friendships, and knowing that if they ever want to talk more, they can.

As much as I would like the positive things in my life to positively affect my friends, I truly appreciate my friendships for what they are, not for what I can get out of my friends or even what I think I have to offer them.

If we're friends with people *solely* for the purpose of evangelism, or *solely* for the purpose of converting them to our point of view, I have to wonder if we are, in fact, true friends at all.

True friends give others the space to have their own thoughts and their own convictions—even if those thoughts and convictions differ dramatically from their own. As a friend once told me, "Don't sacrifice others on the altar of your belief."

While I feel passionate about my convictions, and I would love for everyone to choose the path I've chosen, I also try to honor people's free will to make their own decisions in life.

After sharing once with people, I'm still willing to keep talking to them more about my beliefs, especially if God should prompt that. But I also want to honor the genuine friendships that we share, not making it conditional on them accepting what I believe, or my accepting what they believe.

There's something freeing and joyful in relationships that are truly unconditional, even if our intentions are good in wanting our friends to come to our point of view.

I share these stories with you to encourage you to go ahead and share your thoughts and feelings with your family and friends, even on sensitive topics like this, doing so sensitively, and doing so *especially* if you feel strongly that God has opened the door for you to share.

Don't be afraid to tell your friends and family members what you think. That's part of what makes our relationships with one another so genuine, so real, and so meaningful.

At the same time, I want to encourage you to give your friends and family members the space they might need to come to their own conclusions, respecting and honoring their own free will to follow your suggested path or not, just as you might hope that they would respect and honor your own free will to follow their suggested path or not.

I think you'll find something freeing in this approach if you've never tried it before. I realize that each situation will be different, of course, and I can't say that my approach is the best approach or the only approach. But I can say that this approach has helped me to keep doors open for future conversations, and to keep my relationships intact much better than what I have tried in other ways.

The evangelist D.L. Moody was once rebuked by a woman who said, "I don't care much for your method of evangelism."

Moody responded, "I don't care much for my method either. Tell me, what's yours?"

She said, "I don't have one."

To which Moody replied, "Then I like my method better!"

My method may not be *your* method, but I pray you'll try *some* method!

Perhaps you've never shared your thoughts on this subject with anyone else in your life (or perhaps you've never shared your thoughts about Christ with anyone else, either).

If not, could I encourage you to consider doing so?

Maybe God *hasn't* touched you in this area of your life like He has touched me, but I can imagine He *has* touched you in other ways. And I can imagine, if you've read this far into this book, that you, too, know the power of God and know that He can do anything—absolutely anything.

Maybe you have an unshakable faith in God, and in the Word of God as contained in the Bible, and people *need* to hear about your unshakable faith. You may not know all the answers about homosexuality, but by the time you get to the end of this book, I hope you might have a lot more to offer than you did before.

If so, can I encourage you to speak about what you *do* know or write it down so someone else can hear what you have to say? And as you say it, say it with confidence, but say it with honor and respect, honoring and respecting other people's free will just as you would hope they would honor yours.

As my friend said to me before, it's worth repeating here: "Don't sacrifice others on the altar of your belief."

TEEN TALK

Let me tell you another story to encourage you that sharing your thoughts on this subject can be life changing, even among those who *haven't* asked you to share.

I received a phone call one night about 11 p.m., after I had already been in bed for a while. The call came from a pastor I knew well, so I took it.

He had just come upon three teenage boys at his church who were engaged in a gay ménage à trois. The teens and their parents had stayed after an event at the church to wrap up some things, which is when this encounter occurred.

When this pastor called me, the parents were still there, the boys were still there, and the pastor and his wife were still there. They had called to ask if I could come to their church and help walk them through what to do next. Now this was going to be awkward, for sure, for everyone involved!

I drove to his church and walked into the sanctuary where three embarrassed teens sat next to their three sets of puzzled parents who sat next to their wanting-to-help-but-not-sure-what-to-do pastor and his wife. And I was somehow supposed to have all their answers!

Amazingly, God *did* give me some answers that night, and we *were* able to walk through their situation with as much wisdom and grace as possible.

I talked to the group as a whole, then talked to the teens, then talked to the parents and the pastor and his wife. I set up meetings for later in the week with each of the teens one-on-one, plus a follow-up meeting with each set of parents, then another meeting with all of the teens again together. (This is not meant to be a formula; I just thought I'd share how we walked through that awkward situation both that night and in the weeks that followed.)

After hearing their stories and sharing mine, each of the teens said they were eager and willing to follow a different path than the one they were following on the night they were discovered.

In the years that have followed since then, each of those three young men have gone on to marry three wonderful young women, and they're all starting families of their own. As awkward as it was for them to get caught, I can't help but think it was God's grace that allowed it to happen.

Thankfully, in large part due to a pastor who prayed and acted on their behalf and their parents who were willing to walk with them through this critical time of their lives, all of those young men are now living the life which they believe, and I believe, God has called them to live.

Although these teens didn't *ask* for my input, they were still able to take hold of it when it was extended to them, and their lives were changed in the process.

BANNING TEEN TALK?

I've shared this story with you to encourage you that your words and actions *can* make a difference, even with people who *haven't* asked for your help.

But I've also shared this story with you because there has been a movement in recent years to *ban* people from talking to teens like this, preventing them from receiving the same kind of wisdom and support that I was able to give to those families that night.

Here in my own state, a law came up for a vote just a few years ago to ban licensed professional counselors from even *suggesting* to anyone under 18 what I suggested to those boys that night: that they didn't have to be gay if that's not what they wanted for their lives, and that they weren't locked into the feelings or activities that had led them to that point on the night they were discovered.

Under this law, any mental health provider would be required to *withhold* information from anyone under 18 that they were counseling that such a possibility for change existed, even if that young person stated that they wanted help in this way, and even if their parents signed a consent form so the counselor could offer such help.

Furthermore, professional counselors would be banned from even *referring* such clients to someone else who could possibly offer such help or counsel, not even if the client specifically asked for it, or else that professional counselor would be "subject to discipline by the appropriate licensing authorities."

I was shocked that a bill like this had already made it as far as it had.

Even though I'm not a licensed professional counselor, I have seen enough positive changes in people's lives like these three teens—not to mention hundreds of adults, the majority of whom had achieved their goals of not letting their same-sex attractions control their futures if they wanted to pursue a different outcome for their lives.

Some people call this *the right of self-determination*, the right to determine your own future and what it will look like. In some respects, I would call it *free will*.

While this bill was being considered, I heard that the representative from my district was wondering how he should vote on this bill and that he was open to input from his constituents.

I called his office and left a message about the positive changes I had seen in my own life and the lives of many others I knew, including people who were living in his home district.

He promptly called back to talk more, and he listened carefully to what I had to say.

Then he asked, "What about those who say that this type of counseling is *damaging* to people?"

I said, "I've heard some people say that, too, and I'm sure there are people who have been hurt by counseling of *all* kinds in *all* kinds of ways. But in *my* 30 years of talking with hundreds of people who have dealt with same-sex attractions, I have not once found that to be the case. On the contrary, those with whom I have spoken have been genuinely filled with hope, often for the first time in their lives, to hear that they really *do* have an option, that they really *can* live the kind of lives they want to live."

The next day, I was thankful to see that he voted the way I had hoped he would vote, which to me was a simple decision to allow people the right of self-determination.

Unfortunately, the bill passed anyway—and similar bills have been passing in several other states as well—cutting off that right for anyone under 18 from receiving help for something in which they feel trapped and can't find their way out of on their own.

GOD'S IDEA

I find it ironic that the woman who introduced this bill in our state was a lesbian who had spent years fighting for, and winning, the right to pursue the path which she felt was best for her own life, yet now she wanted to restrict *others* from pursuing the path that *they* felt was best for their lives.

If we want others to respect our free will, we need to respect the free will of others. If this woman honestly cared about the mental health of kids, I think that she, of all people, would have *wanted* to offer them the full range of freedoms for which she had fought and won for herself. Instead, she was now sacrificing others on the altar of her beliefs.

While I'm saddened to hear that anyone is ever required to go into counseling to change their sexual pursuits against their will, I am also saddened by restrictions like these that *prohibit* those who truly want help from getting the help they want from those who can provide it— or even getting a referral to someone who could offer such help!

Some people feel it's wrong to restrict the rights of those who *want* to pursue their same-sex attractions, so to me it seems equally wrong to restrict the rights of those who *don't* want to pursue their same-sex attractions, those who genuinely want help in achieving their own goals.

Rather than being damaging, as this representative had asked me about, I have found, based on my own experience and the experience of hundreds of people with whom I have personally spoken, that there have been many, *many* people who have found such conversations and counsel to be helpful, hopeful, and life-giving.

Free will is not just a good idea; it's God's idea.

While God has plans for each of our lives, He still allows us to choose for ourselves whether we will follow His plans or not.

As Joshua told the Israelites: "Now fear the Lord and serve Him with all faithfulness... But if serving the Lord seems undesirable to you, then choose for yourselves this day whom you will serve... as for me and my household, we will serve the Lord" (from Joshua 24:14-15).

MAINTAINING FRIENDSHIPS

While I strongly believe the things I believe, I'm still going to be friends with people who believe differently, even on this topic. I'm okay with that! They're my friends!

Just because my friends and I have different beliefs on certain topics that doesn't hinder me from sharing my thoughts with them. But *because* I'm friends with them, I also don't beat them up over it. I don't post rants against them on social media. I don't send angry articles to them to vent my frustrations at how ludicrous I might think they are for believing what they believe.

Perhaps you take a different approach with your friends. If so, I'm happy to honor your free will to do that, too! I just want to make sure that you've thought through and prayed through your approach, making sure that it honors and respects the free will of those you're trying to reach.

Part of any differences there may be between my approach and the approach of others could be from differences in style or personality or simply keeping track of what's been effective for me and what hasn't been effective. But I wanted to share with you what I do, and what I don't do, because I believe it's entirely possible to have open and civil discussions on topics like these, allowing others to exercise their free will as God has allowed me to exercise mine.

If the words that I'm saying about honoring and respecting the free will of others just sound like grand platitudes, I'm sorry. They're not! And I certainly don't promote the view that all beliefs are equal.

But as I said before, in the marketplace of ideas, I believe that the beliefs I hold can hold their own—and even win the day. That's why I believe there's great value in sharing those ideas.

I also believe, however, that those ideas must be shared with civility and kindness, and with mutual affection and love, especially with those who might be hard to love.

I wish everyone could experience what I've experienced by putting my faith in Jesus. I wish everyone could experience what I've experienced since coming out of homosexuality. But I'm also not going to get bent out of shape if people don't *want* to experience what I've experienced—even as much as I might want that for them. Not everyone *wants* to change.

For some, going back into the closet feels like going back into a cage. For others, having to *keep living* in something which they've never asked for nor desired feels like going back into a cage, too. *No one* wants to feel like they're trapped in a cage. And that's the beauty of free will. No one has to be.

As much as God *could* force everyone to do His will, He's a Gentleman, allowing us to choose for ourselves which path we will follow.

As you talk to your family and friends, my encouragement to you is the same as my encouragement I've given to those to whom I've ministered, and to lawmakers as they try to govern people rightly: to give people the same free will, the same right to determine their own futures, as God has given to you.

Study Guides For Chapters 9 & 10

STUDY GUIDE FOR CHAPTER 9: "A FEW WORDS ABOUT PAIN"

CHAPTER SUMMARY

Pain can drive us to consider doing things we might never have considered doing otherwise. Even Jesus faced some of his most significant temptations on the night before He died.

The author mentions four things that helped him through a time when he was facing some of his own deep pain:

- he asked for prayer,
- he read the Scriptures,
- he went to church,
- and he talked to a friend.

Each of these activities bore fruit as those prayers were answered, the Scriptures came alive, and he was encouraged by his church and his friend.

When the truth finally broke through again, his temptations fled and the darkness lifted. During this time, the author heard one of the best pieces of wisdom he had ever heard regarding same-sex attractions when his pastor said: "If you do something that God says not to do, it won't go well for you."

QUESTIONS FOR REFLECTION & DISCUSSION

Read Luke 22:39-46. What did Jesus tell His disciples to do so they wouldn't fall into temptation? What did Jesus do, when He might have been tempted to do otherwise, to help Him stay true to the path His Father had laid out for Him? How does this passage describe Jesus' very real anguish during that difficult time?

Read James 5:19-20. What does the Apostle James say will happen whenever we help someone turn away from sin?

Why would pain tempt people to consider doing things they might never have considered doing otherwise?

What are some things we can do to safeguard ourselves from our temptations when we're in pain? What can we do for others to help safeguard them from their temptations when they're in pain?

Have you ever known someone who has made a wrong choice regarding their temptations when they were in pain? Have you ever made a wrong choice, or been tempted to make a wrong choice, when you were in pain?

What happens when someone does something that God says not to do? Why is sin *always* a destructive option in the long term, not just a second-best or third-best option?

Have you ever experienced the truth of the statement: "The trouble with trouble is that it usually starts out as a whole lot of fun"? If so, what has been the outcome? How could "thinking your way through" rather than just "feeling your way through" have changed the outcome?

STUDY GUIDE FOR CHAPTER 10: "THE IMPORTANCE OF FREE WILL"

CHAPTER SUMMARY

How do we interact with people who hold onto their deeply held beliefs just as strongly as we hold onto ours? The author makes three suggestions:

- it's still helpful and good to share our beliefs with one another, as that's the way true friends and family members can best learn from one another,
- after sharing with each other our deeply held beliefs, it's also helpful and good to honor other people's free will to choose and to hold their own decisions,
- it's important to keep the door of communication open for future conversations on the topic.

The author says that much of the success he's had in his conversations with those experiencing same-sex attractions is possibly due to the fact that the majority of people with whom he interacts have sought him out. Among those that *he* has approached to discuss this topic, rather than the other way around, he has often found polite listeners, but little change—unless the person really *wants* to change.

While the author notes that others might take different approaches to their conversations on this topic, he also notes that some people take no approach at all. He encourages people to consider at least *some* approach for interacting with their friends and family members on this topic.

The author also tells a story of three young men who *didn't* ask for his help, but whose parents and pastor did, and how God used what he shared to bring about a new direction in their lives.

He adds that while some say it could be damaging to *force* people to change, it seems equally damaging to *restrict* people from getting help to achieve their own goals for their lives, just as many gays have fought for and won the right to pursue and achieve their own goals as well.

The author concludes with the words of a friend which encapsulate how to honor one another's free will by saying, "Don't sacrifice others on the altar of your belief."

QUESTIONS FOR REFLECTION & DISCUSSION

Read 1 Corinthians 13:2. How can this passage apply to our interactions with those who *want* to pursue their same-sex attractions to the fullest? How can we express our love, even when we disagree with something a person does?

Read Joshua 24:15. What does Joshua say in this passage about giving others the freedom to exercise their own free will? What does Joshua say about exercising *his* own free will, regardless of what others might say? How can we apply this principle to our conversations with those we love and with whom we may disagree regarding the decisions we make in our lives?

Although the author was joking about how many psychologists it takes to change a light bulb, what truth might there be in the punchline, "the light bulb has to really want to change"? If people don't want to make changes in their lives, or don't believe that such changes are possible, what are the chances of them actually changing? How might the stories in this book help someone to desire such a change or to believe that such a change is possible?

Have you ever felt *nudged* by God to do something? And, by comparison, have you ever felt *obligated* to do something, but not necessarily nudged? Did you find any differences in the results?

Why might God sometimes want us to share a truth with someone else, even if we don't see any results from doing so?

What did D.L. Moody ask the woman who told him she didn't care for his method of reaching out to others? After hearing her answer, why did he say that he liked his method better? What about you? What method do you have for loving gays that you've found to be effective?

Having read what you've read so far in this book, what ideas have you gotten about loving gays better that you could put into practice?

Having read what you've read so far in this book, what do you think about the idea of lawmakers restricting people who *don't* want to pursue their same-sex attractions from getting help in achieving their goals? What do you think about the idea that teens, in particular, are being prevented now in several states from getting help in this area?

While we might *want* others to experience what we've experienced, and while it can be helpful and good to share our experiences with others, why is it important to let others exercise their own free will in regards to what we're shared? What benefits could come from following the advice: "Don't sacrifice others on the altar of your belief"?

Chapter 11:

The Importance Of Seat Belts

———— ❖ ————

In which I share about the importance of wearing our seat belts—especially now as the pendulum on this issue is swinging so swiftly.

———— ❖ ————

A few months ago, a good friend was encouraging me to pray for whomever God might bring into my life as a possible spouse for the next season of my life.

I noticed, however, that whenever my friend mentioned it, she referred to my future spouse as "your person." "Pray for your person" or "I'm looking forward to meeting your person" or "Maybe your person is someone you already know."

I didn't think much about her wording until I read an article about a woman in a same-sex relationship who described her partner as "my person."

So the next time I talked to my friend, I said, "Whenever you refer to my possible future spouse, I've noticed that you never use the words 'she' or 'her,' but rather 'your person.' I just wanted to check if you're doing that intentionally, and if so, is it because you think 'my person' could really be either a woman *or* a man?"

My friend paused for a moment and thought seriously about my question—which made me pause for a moment and try to fill in the blanks for myself: *"Does she really think, after all she knows about me, that God would now want me to marry a man instead of a woman?"*

Rather than answering me right away, she said she'd like to pray about it for a few days and get back to me.

A few days later, she did. She sent me a note saying, among other sincerely kind things, "I believe that you can have the relationship you want at the depth that you want with any man or woman to whom you are mutually drawn. I am with you. I am for you, whatever your choices may be."

While my friend meant well with her words, and while she knew that what she was saying might be surprising to me, what she didn't know was how, after reading them, I would be so utterly devastated, so entirely deflated, and so completely broken.

It was as if she had negated everything that God had ever spoken to me in my life about this topic; negated the thousands of hours I've spent praying about it; negated the hundreds of conversations I've had with people who have come to me for help to break free from their same-sex attractions; negated the scores of talks I've given and articles I've written and books I've published, each one at a pretty high cost to myself and my family for doing so; negated my marriage to Lana and the births of all six of my children; and negated the most significant and life-changing conversation I've ever had with God in my life—the conversation which caused me to put my faith in Christ and trust in Him fully for everything in my life, including my sexuality.

What deflated me the most was that if *she* didn't believe me, that God has been speaking to me about this topic so clearly and so consistently for over 30 years, who *would* believe me?

I had already had nine other close, Christian friends who had shifted their positions on homosexuality over the past few years. They, like many others in our country, had "evolved" in their thinking, believing that homosexuality was now right and good and something to be celebrated.

Every time a friend has told me that they now embrace homosexuality, I've felt a little more deflated, a little more isolated, a little more alone.

I know my friends don't mean to do it, but they have no idea how hard it is for someone like me to hear what they're saying—someone who has wrestled through this difficult issue for so many years—to hear that those who are closest to you seem to imply that they no longer believe what you've been saying all along, no longer believe that God has been speaking to you, and no longer believe everything you've fought for, fought through, and given up in order to help yourself and help others live their lives a little better, a little freer. It is utterly disheartening.

My friend's suggestion that I could marry whomever I wanted to marry, regardless of their gender, was the final blow. It was a statement that sent me to the ground. I felt like *I* was that deflated beach ball which I had described earlier, and *I* had sunk to the bottom of the ocean with no air left inside me.

To be honest, I didn't know if I could ever write or speak another word on this topic. If my closest friends no longer seemed to believe what I was saying, how could *anyone* believe me?

STANDING UP AGAIN

But what helped me to finally stand up again, to open up my computer and try explaining it—again—was that I knew that my friends who were shifting their positions on this topic weren't shifting because they didn't believe me, at least not directly, but because they were now trying to figure out for themselves how best to love those around them who are experiencing same-sex attractions.

I also knew that *many* people to whom I had personally ministered *had* believed me, and *still* believed me, and their lives are a reflection of the truth I've been speaking for all these years.

I know too many people whose lives have been entirely transformed by the words I've shared about my own transformation. I've seen God work in my life and in the lives of others in such powerful ways that I *know* He'll continue to work in still more lives in still more powerful ways.

I also know it's not up to me to change people's hearts or lives or beliefs on this topic, but in the end, it's up to God Himself—only He can do such a thing.

As the Apostle Paul said: "My message and my preaching were not with wise and persuasive words, but with a demonstration of the Spirit's power, so that your faith might not rest on men's wisdom, but on God's power" (1 Corinthians 2:4-5).

Even *my* faith didn't come from Paul's words alone, but from a demonstration of the Spirit's power as God brought those words to life for me.

As I literally lay there on the floor, off and on for a few days straight, the words that kept coming to me over and over were the same words the blind man spoke after His own healing: "One thing I do know. I was blind, but now I see!" (John 9:25b).

I knew that my friend didn't mean to hurt me or crush me or deflate me. I knew, and very much appreciated, that she was trying to express how much she loved me, how much she was *for* me, and how much she would *support* me no matter what I chose to do.

ANOTHER DEEP DIVE

So after getting over the initial shock of her words, I decided to go back to God once again and ask Him if there was anything more He wanted to say to me on this topic—anything more that He wanted me to hear.

I'm not so conceited to think that I've plumbed the full depth of what God has to say on this topic, or any other topic, to not keep coming back to Him again and again for *more*. Even though I had talked with God numerous times about this over the years, I took this opportunity to revisit everything that God had spoken to me in the past and anything further He might want to say to me now.

The result of that time of "revisiting" with God is this book that you're reading now.

The truth is, the landscape *has* shifted significantly on this issue in recent years, not just here in the U.S., but around the world as well. The landscape has *also* shifted in my personal world, now that I find myself single again and wondering what the future might hold for me in regards to another potential, life-long relationship.

I decided to use my friend's words as a springboard to clarify where possible, and to adjust where necessary, my own thoughts on this issue.

This exercise has once again proven invaluable to me, and for that I am very thankful for the words of my friend, as hard as they were to hear. I've shared my thoughts with her personally just as I'm sharing them with you. She didn't mean any harm, which I already knew. She just wanted to be supportive of me, whatever I might do.

I've already shared with you many of the conclusions I've reached on this topic up to this point. I'd like to share with you here some of the clarifications and adjustments I've learned on this recent deep dive into what I believe to be God's will on this issue, as I hope these thoughts will be helpful to you, too.

A NEW LANDSCAPE

The truth for me is that some of the barriers which once held me back from pursuing a long-term, gay relationship no longer exist.

I *could* now get married legally to a man if I wanted to. I *could* now be in an open relationship with a man, and be widely accepted if I did so, and even hailed as a hero. I *could* now adopt children legally or father children of my own through a surrogate mother, then raise them together with a gay partner. I *could* now join any of a number of churches who would welcome me and embrace me as an out-and-loud gay man. I *could* now find any number of books which would cast shades of gray onto Scriptures which otherwise seem to be pretty black and white.

Given these new realities in the world, what would I *choose*, I wondered—if I could really choose without any hindrance, without any restriction—that which I *truly* desired in the depths of my being? Would I really *want* to pursue a long-term, gay relationship if that were an option for me? Or would I *rather* pursue a long-term heterosexual relationship, given my innermost thoughts and feelings, and the desires in my heart?

I decided to take a deep dive into those waters as well, as risky as it may have seemed, and here's what I found.

While I can see that marrying either a man or a woman could satisfy *certain* hungers in my heart, they would not satisfy the *same* hungers. For all the talk about marriage equality, marrying a man would *not* be the same as marrying a woman, for each brings something different to the table.

If marrying a man were *equal* to marrying a woman, people would have no preference for marrying one gender over another. It is the very *differences* between men and women that cause people to want to marry someone of the same sex versus someone of the opposite sex. True marriage equality would be blind to the differences between men and women.

But some of those who have fought the hardest for marriage equality are those who are anything but blind to those differences. They want to marry the person of their choice, *precisely because* that person is a man or a woman.

When someone wants to change their gender from one to the other, it's not because they feel that both genders are the same, but because they feel that both genders are, in fact, different, and they prefer to identify with one gender *more* than the other.

Some men want the freedom to dress like women while at the same time denying that any differences exist between the two. But if there were no differences, then it wouldn't matter how they dressed. Some women, likewise, want the freedom to act like men, to live like men, and to be treated like men, while denying that any true differences exist between men and women.

Men and women are *not* the same, and it is their *differences* that makes one gender more attractive than the other to some people.

NATURAL SEX

For me, while I've enjoyed romantic and sexual relationships with men in the past, and I could imagine enjoying such a relationship in the future, the inherent biology of the body parts involved makes me realize that there is something not entirely "natural" about such a relationship.

By this I'm saying that even if I *didn't* take into account what God has to say about sex in the Bible, and I *only* took into account what I could see with my eyes in nature all around me, I can see that the sexual parts in a homosexual act really don't fit together quite right.

One of the primary purposes for which those parts *appear* to be designed would never be fulfilled in a same-sex relationship.

While there are other ways of stimulating those body parts which could be genuinely pleasurable, the truth is that sex between two men or sex between two women will always be, at best, a *simulation* of sex between a man and a woman. At worst, engaging in such activity could cause real damage and real harm.

For instance—and again, not to be graphic, but simply scientific—the walls of the lining of a human vagina are thicker and more elastic than the walls of the lining of a human anus, causing the latter to rupture much more easily during a sexual act. Also, a woman's sexual organ produces its own lubrication when stimulated, as does a man's, meaning that the parts not only fit together better, but more smoothly, whereas the anal canal produces no such lubrication, not even with sexual stimulation.

I could go on to describe the fruitfulness that can occur during heterosexual sex when a sperm and an egg join together versus the unfruitfulness of same-sex sex between two men where sperm is released into an orifice which seems to be so much more clearly designed to excrete waste. I could go on to describe still more, but I won't.

These are just a few of the contrasts between the two types of sexual interaction that I can observe in nature that are enough of an indicator to me that there's something amiss in same-sex sex, that something's not quite right.

This doesn't even take into account the differences between lesbian sex or oral sex or mutual touching of one another's sexual parts in various other ways.

While any of these acts certainly can be pleasurable, and indeed can create a strong degree of intimacy between two people, as far as being natural—meaning according to nature as it presents itself to us, and in regards to at least one of the primary purposes for which the sexual organs even exist—this is why I say that same-sex sex is, at best, a simulation of heterosexual sex, and at worst, can actually be harmful or destructive.

When the Apostle Paul says in Romans 1 that gay sex is "unnatural," I don't believe he's using that word in a way that's pejorative. He's not saying same-sex sex is "disgusting" or "repulsive." He's saying, quite simply, that it goes against the way human sex presents itself to us in nature—regardless of whether we attribute the design of sex to nature or to God.

REMARKABLE SEX

Some people will point out that some animals do, at times, behave homosexually, and that others, like earthworms, are created with both male and female body parts. But I'm not convinced that we should be taking our queues from the animal kingdom regarding our own sexual habits.

As one of my friends says, the female praying mantis, for instance, bites off the head of the male immediately after they mate, then goes on to consume the rest of his body so she'll have food for the new life that will soon grow within her. (While some women may applaud this kind of behavior, I personally don't think it does much for long-term relationship building!)

Sex between a man and a woman is incredibly special, incredibly unique. I don't mean it's just special to me. What I mean is, out of all the creatures on the planet, God has created human beings to make love in a way that no other creature can: face-to-face.

There is not one other creature on the planet that has been given this ability! None. To me, this is astounding!

Sure, we can *try* emulating the mating habits of other creatures, and we might even find pleasure in doing so! But when I look at what God has made available to us as human beings, and the differences between heterosexual sex and same-sex sex, then I try to imagine pursuing a same-sex relationship for life, I can't help but feeling that I would be missing out on something incredibly special and unique which God has made possible for human beings alone.

For me, I want the full-meal deal: the full embrace, face-to-face. (And, when I consider the sex life of the praying mantis, I also would like to still be around the day after our love-making is over!)

CONSULTING THE MANUAL

Aside from this natural, biological, and scientific look at sex, I also believe God is the one who has created our bodies and has given us an "owner's manual" in the form of the Bible to go along with them. God has given us these words to help us to protect and preserve our bodies for the fullest life possible. As the Creator of sex, He is the first and foremost authority to tell us *why* He created sex and *how* to make the best use of it.

Commenting on the powerful nature of sex, the evangelist Billy Graham says, "Sex is the most wonderful thing on this earth, as long as God is in it. When the Devil gets in it, it's the most terrible thing on earth."

I couldn't agree more!

As I mentioned before, as I've looked through the passages in the Bible that specifically address same-sex sexual activity, I personally can't think of any other way that God could have worded His warnings on this matter which would have been any clearer or stronger than the way they are already worded.

This *isn't* because God hates people who have same-sex attractions, nor is it because same-sex sex is so repulsive to God that He can't imagine why anyone would ever *want* to do it, but rather because God knows just how powerful our sexual attractions can be. He created sex! He knows *exactly* why people might want to do things sexually which could be harmful to themselves or to others.

God *doesn't* give us warnings about things which He thinks people would never want to do. He gives us warnings about things He *knows* we might do, because He *knows* how powerful those feelings and emotions and attractions can be. God warns us, truly, because He wants us to enjoy these gifts in the most life-giving way possible.

Not heeding God's warnings would be like my children not heeding mine when I tell them not to run into the street because they might die by doing so—then telling them the same thing, several more times in several more ways. Imagine my frustration to find that they were *still* running into the street anyway, suggesting that they felt my instructions were somehow unclear, or that I wasn't really that serious about them.

There are enough words that are clearly recorded in the Bible for me to believe that God *really* doesn't want me to engage in gay sex. And again, in the words of my pastor who spoke to me in such a helpful way on a day when I was very much needing to hear what God had to say on this topic: "If you do something that God says not to do, it won't go well for you."

INTERNAL MOTIVATION

If I had *nothing* holding me back—no family, no church, no ministry, no argument from nature, no Scriptures, no personal revelations from God—I *could* see myself truly enjoying a romantic and sexual relationship with *either* a man or a woman. I really could. And because I *have* enjoyed both types of relationships in the past, I can imagine enjoying either type of relationship again in the future, even though, as I stated before, each type of relationship would meet *different* needs in my life for *different* reasons.

But as I've looked deeper into the depths of my being, I've found this: while I could imagine enjoying a same-sex relationship in the short term, I would enjoy it at my own peril.

What I want most of all, and what I *know* will bring me the most abundant life possible, is a long term, committed relationship with someone of the opposite sex—someone who is a true complement to the strong masculinity that I feel coursing through my being.

I don't feel this way because the Bible tells me so or society tells me so or my family and friends tell me so. I feel this way because I believe God has written it on my heart. He has encoded it in my DNA, within every cell of my being. I am a man, created by God to be intimate with a woman.

Knowing this truth, from the depths of my being, *is incredibly freeing!*

The *ultimate* reason I would want to pursue an opposite sex relationship in the future is not due to any *external* factor telling me so. The reason I would want to pursue such a relationship *is because it is written on my heart to do so.*

As the Bible says: "They show that God's law is not something alien, imposed on us from without, but woven into the very fabric of our creation. There is something deep within them that echoes God's yes and no, right and wrong" (Romans 2:14-15, MSG).

EXTERNAL RESTRAINTS

I love being motivated internally, rather than externally. Yet I'm also thankful for the external restraints. Why? Because while my conscience can tell me what's right and wrong, my conscience is not infallible.

As one pastor writes: "The problem with conscience is that, of all the sources of finding truth, it is the least reliable, because the Bible teaches us that our conscience can be weakened. It can be warped. It can be hardened.... In fact, it can be killed... Just because my conscience lets me get away with something doesn't mean it's right. Every person around the world has been hard-wired to know what is right and what is wrong. The trick is to fill our minds and hearts with God's truth so that we 'echo His yes and no.'"

This is the reason external restraints are so helpful. And this is why I'm so thankful for the evidence I see for heterosexuality in nature and for God's warnings which are recorded in the Bible. This is why I'm so thankful for my family and my friends and my church for genuinely wanting to keep me on God's best path for my life.

I saw a sign on the highway recently which said: "No seat belts? What's holding you back?" I thought it was a fitting analogy for this discussion about sexual encounters, as well as *all kinds* of experiences in which we might want to engage.

If I had *nothing* holding me back, there are plenty of things I would enjoy doing, at least for a time, like jumping off a 100-foot cliff or eating an entire pan full of brownies or seeing if my car really can go 160 miles per hour as it says on its speedometer. And, I'll admit, I've attempted to do some of those things, at least to some degree, having known full well the very real risk that things could have ended quite badly for me!

But living life without *any* restraints is as crazy as riding a roller coaster without first putting on the safety harness which has been specifically designed for it. Just because we *can* do something, doesn't mean we *should* do something.

After Bill Clinton's infamous affair with one of his White House interns, he was asked by a reporter why he did it. Bill responded, "I think I did something for the worst possible reason—just because I could. I think that's just about the most morally indefensible reason that anybody could have for doing anything, when you do something just because you could."

Free will is only free if you're still alive to exercise it. Yes, God has given us *free will*, but what He *hopes* for us is that we'll choose *His* will because He knows that *His* will is always the best for us in the end.

While I'm extremely grateful to God that He has given me free will, I'm also extremely grateful that He has given me the wisdom and ability to restrain myself from doing *absolutely everything* I could *ever* possibly want to do—because there are a *lot* of things I would want to do if I had no restraints. But I know that it wouldn't go well for me if I did those things, just as I know it wouldn't go well for those around me or for the purposes for which God created me.

Why am I telling you all these secret desires that I found in the depths of my heart? Because I want you to know that I have considered these things deeply now for many, many years.

And every time I have emerged from one of these deep dives—*every time*—I have emerged with a greater understanding of why God has said what He's already said on this subject, and why I'm so glad I listened to Him all those years ago.

NEW TERRITORY

Having said all that, I also want to say that while I was on my recent dive into the depths of my being regarding my thoughts, feelings, and desires, I discovered that there is still *much* more territory which I *can* explore in regards to my friendships with men, territory which is *not* sexual or romantic, but territory from which I have held myself back in the past for fear of being thought of as "gay."

While the landscape on this topic *has* shifted, that shift is not necessarily for the worse. In some ways, that shift has made things so much better, even for me.

I think it's important to note, especially for younger readers of this book, why this shift in the landscape hasn't taken place quite as quickly as you might think it *should* have in the hearts and minds of many people in my generation and older.

The fear of having someone think you might be gay is based on the reality that homosexuality was, when I was growing up, actually *illegal*.

A person could be fined, be sent to jail, lose their job, get kicked out of the military, get kicked out of their apartment, be forced into therapy, and otherwise marked for life in the eyes of society—let alone in the eyes of anyone who might possibly consider such a person as a potential spouse.

For these and other reasons (like the desire *not* to get beat up after gym class), I and many others like me, avoided talking openly about our same-sex attractions—ever.

We avoided any appearances of having same-sex attractions at all costs, even steering clear of those who said they *did* have such attractions.

I've realized in recent years, however, that many of those fears that I had when I was younger are no longer valid or helpful. Because of this, God has been showing me ways in which I've *still* been holding back in some of my own thinking and friendships because of fears I've had about how I *appeared*—not because of anything that *God* has said regarding my activities.

For instance, when I recently asked one of my daughters to paint a cover for one of my books, she painted the background in a beautiful shade of purple. To me, however, and because the book was so personally revealing about my own life and walk of faith, her choice of color was the equivalent of me screaming, at the top of my lungs, "Look at me! I'm gay!"

Of course, God has nothing to say in His Word that would *restrict* our use of *any* color, let alone purple. Purple was, in fact, so costly to create in the past that it was often the preferred color of royalty.

As I sat back and thought about my daughter's color choice more rationally, rather than emotionally, I realized that her cover looked absolutely beautiful just the way she had made it. My daughter thought nothing about it, and I knew that it probably wouldn't matter these days even if some people *did* think I was gay (and some people, even among my friends, might have thrown a party for me if they thought I *was* gay).

The fact that I hesitated after first seeing her cover, and the fact that I finally embraced it as beautiful after all, spoke volumes to me about the fact that it is now actually *okay* for me to embrace some of those things which I had once been afraid to embrace. I can embrace them because there is nothing inherently illicit or ungodly about them at all.

In another example, I recently took a selfie with a couple for whom I had performed their wedding.

As I held up the camera, the groom leaned toward me, but the bride didn't, resulting in a picture which showed two men in suits leaning together, while the bride stood upright and off to the side.

I asked if we could retake the picture, saying that the lighting didn't look quite right, which *was* true, but that wasn't the *only* reason I wanted to retake it. I wanted to retake it because, to me, it looked as if the groom and I were the couple, not the groom and his bride.

When I later looked at that first picture we had taken together, it was totally fine! We looked like good buddies who were hanging out at a wedding.

No one would have thought twice about the way we were standing except for me, nor would someone have somehow mistaken that he and I were a couple! But in my hypersensitivity to *appearing* gay in *any* way, I was about to delete an otherwise perfectly normal picture.

NEW ROLE MODELS

The examples go on and on. Since my wife died, I've taken a renewed interest in some of the activities I loved doing when I was younger, like dancing and painting and writing music and playing the piano. I had set aside many of those activities when I first left homosexuality because to me they seemed gay.

In my circle of friends growing up, women dominated arts like these. But over time, I've discovered that a large number of men, both in biblical times and living today, enjoy and excel at doing things like these all the time.

King David, for instance, is known for killing thousands in battle, yet he played the harp and wrote most of the songs in the book of Psalms. But I doubt anyone who ever faced him on the battlefield ever asked him to pull out his Man Card first. Even *he* could make Chuck Norris quiver in his boots.

I've loved playing the piano for many years, as well as the flute and several other instruments, but I've never felt quite "manly" about doing so. But when I read in the Bible about a man named Jubal, way back in Genesis, Chapter 4, I saw that he was called "the father of all who play the flute and harp" (from Genesis 4:21).

Here was a man who not only played the flute *and* the harp, but who was called the "father" of everyone else who would. What an honor! What a distinction! Yet here I had been embarrassed all these years about some of the talents which God had put within me.

King David danced before the Lord (see 2 Samuel 6:14), and a man named Bezalel was skilled at making artistic designs and all types of crafts (see Exodus 31:1-5).

The list of manly role models goes on and on, as recorded both in and out of the Bible. Yet I had pushed back enjoying many of these things for years for fear of being labeled as gay.

RECLAIMING TALENTS

Now, however, I'm thoroughly enjoying playing the piano, not only for myself, but publicly as well. I've been composing music and even writing a musical about the life of the real St. Nicholas who lived back in the 3rd and 4th centuries A.D.

I've been painting pictures for fun and taking dance classes just because they make me laugh.

None of these things are inherently gay. None of these things make me want to have sex with a man! None of these things are restricted by God!

But I'm now beginning to enjoy them more fully because my fear of being *labeled* as gay is finally fading, thanks, at least in part, to society's more accepting views of homosexuality. Being thought of as gay simply no longer carries the same kind of risk as it did 30 years ago.

God has been showing me that I can now start taking down some of the walls that I've put up around my life for protection—walls which are no longer needed.

As I said in the opening chapters, while some people might be put off by society's shift on this issue, there *are* reasons to be very thankful for that shift, as it's finally allowing people (including me) to explore and recapture some of their God-given talents, gifts, and abilities which they may have shunned for a long, long, time—many of which should never have been shunned in the first place.

To conclude this chapter, let me reiterate that it's just plain smart to wear seat belts while driving; it's just plain smart to exercise restraint on activities which are romantic or sexual in order to protect the precious intimacy that God has in mind for us.

But it's also just plain smart to throw off those things which would hinder us from exploring all the territory that's available to us— territory in which we can enjoy our friendships more fully and make use of our God-given gifts, talents, and abilities more fruitfully.

While this changing landscape has produced new freedoms for many, it has also produced new dilemmas, particularly for Christians, which I'll address in the next chapter.

Chapter 12:

The Importance Of Tears

———— ❖ ————

In which I share how tears can be one of your best expressions of genuine love—and how tears can help you to continue loving others while still holding fast to what you believe.

———— ❖ ————

The changing landscape regarding homosexuality has created a need for a genuine response from Christians. I am hoping this book is part of that response.

The very real dilemma which Christians are facing is perhaps best exemplified by the questions surrounding the topic of gay marriage. This is where the proverbial rubber meets the road.

I've noticed that when someone is invited to attend a gay wedding, it suddenly brings to the surface everything that person has ever believed, or thought they've believed, about homosexuality. The couple who has sent the invitation is asking for a response, and the answer that's given has the potential to make or break a friendship for years to come. While it doesn't *have* to be this way, it often *seems* this way for everyone involved.

The dilemma is magnified exponentially when that invitation comes from someone who is very near and dear, such as a son or daughter, a brother or sister, or a close friend or coworker.

How we as Christians respond at times like these really matters. While this chapter focuses on the topic of how you might respond to someone who invites you to a gay wedding, please note that I'm using this as just one example to help you think through how you might truly love God and love gays more deeply, and how you might express your love in a way those you love can receive it.

My hope is that this thoughtful discussion will apply not only to a one-day event, but will also give you some solid help as you continue interacting with and expressing your love toward your gay friends and family members on an ongoing basis.

Let me start with this unchanging truth, which is the overarching goal of any response we could possibly give, and that is *love*. As the Bible says, "...and whatever you do, do it with kindness and love" (1 Corinthians 16:14, TLB).

I'd also like to add up front another important truth. Whenever anyone asks us to do *anything*, it's important to note that love doesn't always say "Yes," but love doesn't always say "No," either. Love takes into account the individuals involved and the unique relationships that exist between those individuals.

I have six children, and I don't always respond the same way to each one, even if they're asking me the exact same question. Why? Because each of them has their own unique personality, and I have a unique relationship with each of them based on their unique personalities, as well as our unique histories of interacting with one another over many years.

Whereas some people will respond well to tough love, others will respond better to simple kindness. The Bible says there's a place for both (see 2 Corinthians 7:8-10 and Romans 2:1-4).

Let's start with the example I used in the previous chapter, where I mentioned a friend who was trying to express her love to me by telling me she would support me no matter what choice I might make in the future regarding the sex of any potential life mate.

While my friend *intended* for her words to be extremely loving, what she didn't realize was how those words would crush me so thoroughly. We don't always know how someone will react to our expressions of love until *after* we've expressed them, because people are not two-dimensional cardboard cutouts who are always entirely predictable!

In the situation with my friend, we took time, a few days later, to talk through how her words made me feel, to hear again what she was really trying to express, and to offer one another our genuine apologies both for being offended on my part, and for causing me to feel anything but loved, as a friend, on her part. I've had to do the same with her on other occasions, when I've said things that *I've* intended to be loving, but were received much differently than intended.

Just because you are friends with someone doesn't mean you can always read their minds, and it doesn't mean that you get it right every time. Thankfully, grace is not a one-time shot, but something we can extend and receive continually.

Remember, "Feelings are everywhere—be gentle."

EXPRESSING OUR THOUGHTS

My point here is that when we're trying to express our love better, it's important to take into account not only *what* we say and do, or even *how good* our intentions might be behind what we say and do, but *how those we love will receive what we say and do.*

Regarding the issue of gay marriage, let's say, for instance, that you believe gay marriage isn't good, right, or healthy for the couple who has invited you to attend their wedding. How does *love* guide your response?

If you believe that what they're doing is not good, right, or healthy, and you feel *prompted by God or by your own inner desire* to share your concerns with one or both of the people getting married, then by all means, please do it!

Do it in love, but don't hold back if you truly feel your words could be helpful to them. I know *I* would have wanted someone to lovingly warn *me* before my wedding day if someone truly thought there was a reason why I shouldn't be marrying the person I was planning to marry. This wisdom applies, of course, whether or not the couple getting married is of the same sex or the opposite sex.

On the other hand, if God *isn't* prompting you to share your concerns with the couple involved or you *don't have* an inner compulsion to do so, then you might want to pay attention to whatever you're sensing or not sensing. It might not be something that God intends for you to bring up or it might not be the right time for you to bring it up or it might make matters worse for everyone involved, both in the short run and in the long run.

There have been times when I have felt *prompted* to say something to someone who was doing something that I have felt was harmful to themselves, but there are other times when I have simply felt *obligated* to say something, not necessarily prompted. The difference between how the recipient received my words was noteworthy, in a positive way in the former case, and a negative way in the latter.

It's not your obligation to right *every* wrong you see in the world. As I've said earlier, God didn't send Jesus "to condemn the world, but to save the world through Him" (John 3:17b). There's a world of difference between condemning people for their sin and saving people from their sin.

Any parent knows that you don't correct children *every* time they do something you believe is wrong or else their children would be in a constant state of fear from ever attempting to do *anything* again. Thankfully, God, in His great mercy, doesn't rebuke me every single time I do something that could potentially be harmful to me. But there *are* times when the stakes are so high that it's important to speak out.

If you decide this is one of those times, I would suggest following the advice of the Apostle James, who says, "Everyone should be quick to listen, slow to speak and slow to become angry..." (James 1:19b). This is in line with how God Himself approaches each of us as well (see Exodus 34:6-7).

TIME, PRAYER, AND DEEP THOUGHT

Some friends of mine were invited to attend a gay wedding a few years ago and asked for my thoughts on what they should do. The wedding was going to be a family reunion of sorts, with relatives attending from several states who hadn't seen each other in quite some time.

My friends' initial reaction was that they shouldn't go, because they didn't believe gay marriage was right. Even though they wanted to go for the sake of their relationships with the couple who had invited them and the rest of the extended family who would be attending, they didn't feel, in good conscience, that they could attend.

"What should we do?" they asked me.

I told them that their initial reaction was certainly a reasonable one, as no one should feel forced to attend or take part in something which they feel violates their conscience.

I also asked them to take some time with their decision, however, not making it too lightly or quickly, as their relationships with the couple and with their extended family were also significant.

So my friends did give it some time, some prayer, and some deep thought. In the end, they still decided not to attend. One of their main reasons for declining was that they felt they couldn't participate in a celebration of something which they believed would actually be harmful to the couple involved.

They also felt their attendance would indicate that they were giving their approval to something of which they believed God did not approve, violating the biblical warning in the book of Romans against giving such approval, which says "...they not only continue to do these very things but also approve of those who practice them" (Romans 1:32b).

My friends didn't make a scene about their decision. The couple who had invited them already knew what my friends believed about gay marriage, so my friends didn't feel the need to say anything more. They politely responded and declined the invitation.

I appreciated that my friends gave it some time, some prayer, and some deep thought regarding their response. The people who had invited them were worthy of that honor.

While the couple getting married *could* have taken offense at my friends' decision, I also believe the couple could have also been genuinely *relieved* by the response. Most couples wouldn't want those they've invited to feel *obligated* to come to their wedding if they didn't feel comfortable in doing so.

I know *I* wouldn't want someone else to violate *their* conscience in order to do something I asked them to do, just as I believe *they* wouldn't want me to violate *my* conscience to do something they asked me to do. Love goes both ways in a relationship, and honoring one another's consciences is one way to express our love.

I can also say that I've been invited to a few weddings over the years where attending wouldn't have violated my conscience, but where I have been less than enthusiastic to attend. Why? Because I'm honestly concerned for the couple getting married. I'm uncertain if their marriage will last even a few months, let alone a few years.

It's a struggle for me to attend such weddings, but I still pray about attending each one regardless, because those who have invited me are worthy of that honor. In the end, my attendance isn't always a reflection of my belief in the couple's relationship with one another; it's a reflection of my belief in the relationship I have with the person who has invited me.

There's a principle here that is perhaps best illustrated by a personal example.

HARMING RELATIONSHIPS

Unfortunately, I know what it's like to be on the receiving end of someone's refusal to attend a wedding—*my* wedding—and I know how that refusal can cause a rift in a relationship that can last for years.

There was a woman who was very close to Lana who sincerely felt Lana was going to go to hell for marrying me, because I grew up in a different denomination than Lana did. This woman said she was praying every day that she could see the good in me, but that she saw only evil. She refused to come to our wedding, hoping that her refusal would cause Lana to call it off.

While Lana appreciated this woman's concern, Lana had her own strong, deeply held beliefs about the issue and felt that marrying me was exactly what God wanted her to do.

This woman went out of her way to express her opinion to Lana on multiple occasions, and Lana tried to politely express hers, but to no avail. There came a point where this woman's regular, vocal refusals were clearly no longer welcome, no longer loving, and no longer kind.

While I mentioned before that I would *want* someone to express to me if they thought I was making a decision about my life that could be a terrible mistake, I also believe there comes a point where such input is no longer helpful, loving, or kind.

If, after I had given someone else's ideas some time, some prayer, and some deep thought of my own, and we still disagreed, I would hope we could reach a place of mutual respect for one another's deeply held beliefs.

Unfortunately, this was *not* the case with this woman who regularly and vocally refused to come to our wedding. While she eventually *did* decide to come to our wedding at the last minute, her words, her actions, and the strife they created between her and Lana created a very real division between them that lingered for *years*.

I believe there's another way, a better way.

A TIME FOR EVERYTHING

As the Bible says, "There is a time for everything, and a season for every activity under heaven... a time to be silent and a time to speak..." (Ecclesiastes 3:1 and 3:7).

There really is a time for everything. There really is a time to be silent and a time to speak. While I appreciated this woman sharing her deeply held beliefs with Lana, when it reached the point that her words simply sounded like "a noisy gong or a clanging cymbal," I wished she would have gotten the hint that what she was doing was no longer loving, but actually quite damaging.

On the other hand, I am glad she voiced her opinions *prior* to the wedding, rather than during the ceremony itself!

I've wondered what someone might do if the officiant at a gay wedding were to ask the once-common question: "If anyone knows of any reason why this couple shouldn't be united in marriage, let them speak now or forever hold their peace."

Would that be the time for someone who has a deeply held belief that gay marriage is wrong to speak up and expound on why they think the couple shouldn't get married? Or is there a better way? A better time?

If someone waited until that point in the ceremony to speak, I believe that would be *incredibly* unkind and unloving. I mention this because if God *is* prompting you to speak to the couple, I would hope you would do it *prior* to the wedding day, not in the middle of their ceremony! Remember, "whatever you do, do it with kindness and love."

Perhaps a phone call or a conversation over coffee with one or both of the people who have invited you would be appropriate. Or if getting together in person seems too awkward or potentially explosive, perhaps a card or a letter would work well.

Or, perhaps as I mentioned earlier, if God *isn't* prompting you to say something, and you *don't* feel an inner compulsion to do so, it could be worth heeding that lack of prompting or inner compulsion as well. Just as there really are appropriate times to speak, there really are appropriate times to be silent.

If you feel you should say something, please don't let any of this discourage you from doing so (read again James 5:19-20). But also don't feel obligated to say something if God *isn't* calling you to say something, or else your words might just sound like a noisy gong or a clanging cymbal. This is why it's so important to give your response some time, some prayer, and some deep thought.

MAINTAINING RELATIONSHIPS

I've also talked with people who have been invited to gay weddings by those very close to them who have taken a different approach to expressing their love, feeling like God has prompted them to attend.

I've listened to their heartfelt considerations over what they should do or should not do. I've watched as they've wrestled with their feelings of wanting to be there for those they love, yet not wanting to see any harm come to them, either.

How does someone decide what to do when they are feeling prompted by God to attend? Again, I believe it's important to give it some time, some prayer, and some deep thought. I also have to remember that while love doesn't always say "Yes," it doesn't always say "No," either.

As I mentioned earlier, my attendance at a *straight* wedding isn't always a reflection of my belief in the relationship of the couple getting married, but a reflection of my belief in my relationship with the person who has invited me.

For some who have made this immense decision, they have found there's wisdom in attending for this very reason: to maintain their relationships with those who have invited them.

When those who have been invited have close relationships with the couple who has invited them, and everyone already knows each other's deeply held beliefs on the subject, there isn't any confusion that their attendance might indicate approval. Rather, their attendance indicates their willingness to maintain their relationships with those they love—even when they disagree.

GOD'S KINDNESS

Walking alongside those we love while they do things which we strongly believe is harmful and destructive to them is probably one of the hardest things any of us ever has to do.

I can also imagine this is one of the hardest things *God* ever has to do for *us*, allowing us the freedom to exercise our own free will when He knows full well where some of our decisions will lead.

Yet, walking alongside us in this way is also one of the most *loving* things God does for us—even when we're making decisions that are permanent, life-altering, and potentially very harmful. God promises us that He will still be right there with us, letting us exercise our own free will—even if He has to fight back tears while we do it.

As God says in the Bible: "Never will I leave you; never will I forsake you" (Hebrews 13:5).

I've tried to think how many times God has walked alongside *me* when *I've* chosen to do things which go against His will, things which were destructive to me as well as to those around me.

I've tried to think about how many *tears* God must have shed as I've done those things, yet He has still walked beside me all along the way. As a parent, I've shed a fair number of tears of my own on behalf of those I love, as I've walked alongside them through some very difficult things as well. But I can also say that our genuine tears can often speak more meaningfully than any words we could ever say.

Tears really are one of the greatest expressions of love we can offer on behalf of those we love. As Washington Irving said, "There is a sacredness in tears. They are not the mark of weakness, but of power. They speak more eloquently than ten thousand tongues. They are the messengers of overwhelming grief, of deep contrition, and of unspeakable love."

I recently spoke at the funeral of a dear friend and one of the godliest women I know. One of her grandsons came up to me after the funeral to tell me just how much his grandmother's life had impacted his own.

He told me of how, when he was a young teenager, one of the gifts he wanted for Christmas one year was an album of music which was one of the most vulgar available. He was in a time of rebellion himself, and the music gave expression to all the pain that he felt and the anger that he wanted to convey to the world around him.

He cried as he told me the story of how his grandmother had given him the album that he had requested that Christmas, and as she did so, she started a conversation with him about what he was feeling and why. She told him she understood why he was wanting that music, but that there was a better way to deal with what he was feeling—that he didn't have to turn to that music for help, but he could turn to God.

She was willing to meet him where he was, but she wasn't willing to leave him there. By giving him the album, she expressed her love in a way that he could receive it. But she also pointed him to another way, a better way.

I cried as I listened to what my dear friend had done, something which I'm not sure I could have done, yet something which had so touched this young man's life that a few months after receiving that album, he gave his life completely to Christ and gave up seeking his solace in things which would ultimately destroy him.

I can't suggest my friend's approach to every person in every situation, but I *can* say that God used her approach that day in a powerful way to touch this young man's life. And because my friend was such a strong woman of God, I am confident that she had given her decision some time, some prayer, and some deep thought before proceeding in the direction she felt led to proceed.

MY TEARS

How does this relate to gay marriage? It relates because God used this story to bring me to tears one night when I felt He was asking me if *I* could ever attend a gay marriage some day if, for some particular reason, He really *wanted* me to attend.

Although I have walked alongside others as they've made their decisions about whether to attend a gay wedding or not, I've never been asked to attend one myself. But one night God asked me to consider what I would do if I were invited by someone I dearly loved. It's one thing to counsel others as *they* try to navigate these rocky waters. It's another thing when *you're* the one in the boat.

While it's hard to hypothesize without knowing the specifics, I do think there's value in thinking through this issue *before* being asked, so that we'll be better prepared to answer if or when we *are* asked.

Could *I* attend a gay wedding, knowing what I know about homosexuality and believing what I believe about what God has spoken to me so clearly on this topic?

The dilemma for me is that my involvement with homosexuality almost killed me. It is *the* sin in my life which God pointed out to me as the reason Jesus gave up His life for me. I was headed toward death, but Jesus said He had paid that price for me already. If I was willing to put my faith in Him, I could gain back my life and live with Him, and for Him, forever.

While there were many other sins in my life for which Jesus died and which He later pointed out to me, this was the one that God highlighted for me out of all the sins listed in Romans Chapter 1. This is what led me to put my faith in Christ in the first place.

I couldn't see how I could ever attend a ceremony which would solemnify a relationship for which I believe Jesus had to go to the cross. I just couldn't.

But God seemed to be asking me—almost like He might have done when He asked Abraham to sacrifice his son Isaac on an altar—if I would be willing to go to a gay wedding if God Himself were to prompt me to do so.

The thought of it drove me to tears—just as the thought of Abraham having to sacrifice his son must have driven Abraham to tears. What would *I* do if someone near and dear to me invited me to their gay wedding, even if they knew my deeply held beliefs, yet they still wanted very much for me to be there on one of the most significant days of their lives?

All I could do was to cry; cry for the permanence of the decision someone close to me would be making; cry for the harms that could come to my loved one as a result; cry for this decision which would be closing the door forever to the possibility of their marrying someone of the opposite sex like I had married Lana and experienced something with her that was beyond anything I ever could have imagined.

But then I thought of how many buckets full of tears God has cried over me when I've made decisions that have impacted me for the rest of my life—and how He walked alongside me still, holding my hand, all along the way.

Sure, I could stay home and pretend it wasn't happening. Or I could attend and sit miserably in the corner, as if I were wearing a black arm band in protest for feeling coerced into attending. Or maybe there was a better way.

Maybe, as God was suggesting to me, I could hold the hand of my loved one on one of the most significant days of their lives, not because of my belief in the relationship between the couple getting married, but because of my belief in my relationship with my loved one who had invited me.

"Maybe I could, God," I said, "but only after shedding many, many tears."

And God said, "Now you're beginning to understand the depths of My love. You're beginning to understand how I can do what I have to do on a daily basis as well. You're beginning to understand how I can show grace to millions, even while they're in the midst of their sins, knowing what their sins will cost them—because I know what their sins have cost Me."

As the Bible says, "But God demonstrates His own love for us in this: While we were still sinners, Christ died for us" (Romans 5:8).

TAKING IT TO HEART

If you remember my story at the beginning of this book about my dear friend and like-minded believer who stopped reading my book at one point in Chapter 12, and who sent me a note saying she couldn't read any more? *This* is that point.

I didn't explain it quite as carefully as I'm explaining it to you now. And I still might not be capturing it exactly as God explained it to me. But after she read the first draft of my book, where I said I could see myself possibly attending a gay wedding if God were to prompt me and if my relationship with the person who had invited me was of the utmost importance, my friend wondered how I could ever attend a gay wedding, for any reason, under any circumstance.

She said that it felt like I was contradicting everything I had said in the rest of the book, because it sounded to her like I was endorsing gay marriage. But my words in that draft must have been muddier than I expected, because nothing could be further from the truth. I cannot celebrate, I cannot endorse, I cannot affirm something which God does not celebrate, endorse, or affirm. I cannot.

The truth is, I believe that what God showed me that night served to highlight and underscore *everything else I've said in the rest of this book* about what it takes to love God and love others to the fullest extent possible.

What had he shown me? He had shown me the importance of tears—tears expressing themselves in love.

Could I attend a gay wedding? Not with celebration. But perhaps I could go out of respect for my relationship with the person who had invited me. I couldn't celebrate something for which Jesus had to go to the cross. Perhaps I could possibly go if going was a way to express my true affection toward the person who had invited me *in a way that person could receive it*—just as my friend who had given her grandson an album had expressed her true affection to him in a way he could receive it. While the stakes might be higher in attending a gay wedding, I can see how the same principle would allow those I love to hold onto their deeply held beliefs, while I held onto mine.

There's a world of difference between walking alongside someone in celebration of something which is harmful to them and walking alongside someone while holding back tears. Outwardly, both approaches might look exactly the same. But inwardly, the difference is in the tears—tears expressing themselves in love.

Someone might say, "Then wouldn't it be better to not go at all?"

I would think so, too, except for God's reminder to me of the many times in my life when *He* has walked alongside *me* through things which I know He wished He would never have had to walk through with me at all. Looking back on those times now, all I can say is that I'm so thankful that He did.

Would I *want* to attend a gay wedding? No, I wouldn't want to attend, as I sincerely believe that God has warned us not to engage in homosexual acts, and I sincerely believe, "If you do something God says not to do, it won't go well for you." And *because* of my beliefs, I can't imagine most couples would *want* me to attend their weddings, either. No one wants to force someone to do something they believe the other person doesn't want to do.

But I *can* see where, if someone's invitation to me *were* to be extended in heartfelt love, knowing fully what I believe on this topic and why, yet still wanting me to attend because of our genuine, mutual affection for one another, then perhaps I could attend—not because I believe in gay marriage, but because I believe in my relationship with the person who has invited me.

As I explained this truth more fully to my friend who had stopped reading this book at this point, and as God began to show her what He had shown me, that's when she called me back to say, "I think I need to take to heart what you're saying in that chapter. There's a truth in there that I think God wants me to see."

There's a time for tough love, to be sure, and God might call you to express your love in that way (see 2 Corinthians 7:8-10). But there's also a time for simple kindness, and God might call you to express your love like that, too (see Romans 2:1-4). Just as the Bible talks about how tough love can lead to repentance, it talks about how kindness can lead to repentance as well.

These are tough decisions, and not ones to be taken lightly. If they were easy, I doubt that you would have even started reading a book like this!

But I am convinced that if you're willing to ask God for His wisdom, giving your decisions enough time, prayer, and deep thought in order to hear from Him, then you can make decisions that will honor Him, honor those you love, and honor your convictions to your own deeply held beliefs.

As the Bible says: "If any of you lacks wisdom, he should ask God, who gives generously to all without finding fault, and it will be given to him" (James 1:5).

THE FULLNESS OF JESUS' WORDS

Before we leave this discussion, there's an important nuance here that I don't want you to miss.

While I have used gay marriage in this chapter as an example of loving others through our tears, it is one of many situations we will all face in life when we'll have to decide how best to express our love to others in a way they can hear it while still holding onto our deeply held beliefs.

I believe Jesus gives us the *best* example for how we can do just that.

A friend of mine recently attended a special event at a church he was visiting. The pastor in charge of the event stood up at one point and read from his Bible the passage about the woman who was caught in adultery and who was brought before Jesus.

The pastor was relating this passage to the issue of homosexuality. Here's what he read:

The teachers of the law and the Pharisees brought in a woman caught in adultery. They made her stand before the group and said to Jesus, "Teacher, this woman was caught in the act of adultery. In the Law Moses commanded us to stone such women. Now what do you say?"

They were using this question as a trap, in order to have a basis for accusing Him.

But Jesus bent down and started to write on the ground with His finger. When they kept on questioning Him, He straightened up and said to them, "If any one of you is without sin, let him be the first to throw a stone at her."

Again He stooped down and wrote on the ground.

At this, those who heard began to go away one at a time, the older ones first, until only Jesus was left, with the woman still standing there.

Jesus straightened up and asked her, "Woman, where are they? Has no one condemned you?"

"No one, sir," she said.

"Then neither do I condemn you," Jesus declared.

(John 8:3-11a).

At that point in the story, the pastor closed his Bible, looked around the room, and said, "That's all I need to hear. We ought to say the same to those who are gay: 'Then neither do I condemn you.'"

My friend said that nearly every head in the room nodded in agreement. Nearly every head, that is, except my friend's. He had kept his Bible open just a little longer to keep reading what Jesus said next.

He wondered why the pastor had closed his Bible at that point in the story, rather than reading the *rest* of what Jesus had said to the woman that day.

Why would the pastor only share *some* of Jesus' words and not the *fullness* of Jesus' words?

What my friend read, and what the pastor *would* have read to the people at that event had he kept his Bible open for just one sentence more, were the following words:

"Go now and leave your life of sin" (John 8:11b).

While I truly believe this pastor and the people in that room might have sincerely given some time, some prayer, and some deep thought to this issue, and had found *some* nuggets of truth, I also believe they stopped short of finding the *fullness* of what Jesus had to say on this topic.

Jesus *did* view the sins of this woman as no different than the sins of the rest of those who had gathered around to stone her. That was true.

And Jesus *did* prove that He didn't want anyone to stone her, but that He wanted her to live and not die. As He told Nicodemus, He really didn't come "to condemn the world, but to save the world" (see John 3:17). That was true, too.

But the nugget of truth that the pastor and these people hadn't yet found was the nugget that would *ensure* this woman wouldn't die from what she was doing, but rather would enable her to live her life to the full. This nugget was contained in Jesus' final words to her: "Go now and leave your life of sin."

It was *this nugget* of truth that would cost Jesus His life only a few days later. It was *this nugget* of truth that was the only reason Jesus could forgive her of her sins and let her go free, for He Himself was headed to the cross to pay the price for her sins with His own life. It was *this nugget* of truth that would allow her to *truly* go free and to *truly* live the life God had created her to live all along.

The Bible doesn't tell us what that woman did with her life after Jesus set her free. But based on what happened to me when I faced the very real possibility of death for *my* sins, and my resulting commitment to *never* go back to my former ways again, I can imagine that she never went back to her previous ways again, either.

God has shown us all His incredible grace, and He wants us to extend that grace to others. He has also shown us His incredible love, and He wants us to extend that love to others as well.

Grace says, "Neither do I condemn you."

Love adds, "Go and sin no more."

My hope is that all of us will keep searching for *every* nugget of truth that God has in mind for us to find, on this topic and on many others, never stopping short of the *fullness* of what He has to say.

As the Bible says, "God wants us to grow up, to know the whole truth and tell it in love—like Christ in everything" (Ephesians 4:15a, MSG).

P.S. Don't miss reading the Conclusion and the Afterword, which follow the study guides on the following pages! Some early readers of this book said these final two chapters are some of their favorites in the whole book!

Study Guides For Chapters 11 & 12

STUDY GUIDE FOR CHAPTER 11: "THE IMPORTANCE OF SEAT BELTS"

CHAPTER SUMMARY

Some Christians want to support and affirm their gay friends by encouraging them to pursue their same-sex attractions to the fullest. But for people who *don't* want to pursue their same-sex attractions, such "support" can be truly crushing. The author suggests that:

- while we all want our friends to love and support us, we don't want them to encourage us to do things that go against our own deeply held beliefs,
- and while we all want to *be* loving and supportive, we must realize that the words of support we offer to others might not *sound* like support to those who hear them.

One person's message of hope might sound like a message of bondage to another. All of this points out why we need to speak carefully and prayerfully on this issue, taking into account the person to whom we're talking.

While many of the restraints that once held people back from pursuing homosexuality no longer exist, the restraint of God's Word has remained unchanged. God's Word acts like a "seat belt" for us and is still the best protection to keep us from harming ourselves and others.

The author says that the changing landscape on this issue:

- has been helpful in some ways for those who are experiencing same-sex attractions as they can now more freely explore valid ways to meet their valid needs without fear of being labeled gay,
- but that none of these new freedoms have changed the fact that men and women *are* different, which is why people still often prefer to marry a person of one sex over another.

Even with all these new freedoms, the author discusses why he is fully convinced that God's Word on this issue is still the best form of restraint: for our sake, for God's sake, and for the sake of everyone involved.

QUESTIONS FOR REFLECTION & DISCUSSION

Read 1 Corinthians 2:4-5. How can our testimony speak as much to people about the power of God as any of the other words we might try to use to convince them of our beliefs? How does the author's testimony speak about the power of God as much as any of the other words he might try to use?

Read John 9:25. What is it about the simple testimony of the blind man whom Jesus had healed that makes it so powerful?

Read Romans 1:26-27. Why would the Bible describe homosexual acts as "unnatural"? What statement does this make about "the facts of life" as presented to us by nature?

Read Genesis 4:21, 2 Samuel 6:14, and Exodus 31:1-5. While some activities might strike people as more or less gay, what does the Bible say about the variety of gifts God has given to His people? How can passages like these give additional freedom to those who are experiencing same-sex attractions to meet their valid needs?

What did the author say about why it deflated him so thoroughly when a friend offered to support him, regardless of the gender of whoever he might marry in the future? How can our words of support, even when lovingly expressed, sometimes still be taken the wrong way?

What words do you think the author might have *wished* his friend had said to him, while still supporting him as a person, but without supporting something which he felt God had strongly warned him against?

How can we offer our genuine love, care, and compassion to those who are experiencing same-sex attractions—without compromising our own deeply held beliefs?

In what ways have you seen public opinion and public policy change on this issue over your lifetime? And in recent years?

How do you think this swing in public opinion and public policy will affect those who are experiencing same-sex attractions as they try to decide for themselves which path they will pursue? Do you think this shift makes their decisions harder or easier?

If gender truly doesn't matter regarding the issue of marriage, why would someone still prefer to marry a person of one sex over another? Can you see how different needs could be met by people of different genders, but not the same needs?

STUDY GUIDE FOR CHAPTER 12: "THE IMPORTANCE OF TEARS"

CHAPTER SUMMARY

The new landscape regarding homosexuality requires a genuine response from the church. The author hopes this book is part of that response. In this chapter, the author uses the example of being invited to attend a gay wedding to address various approaches to expressing our love in other situations as well. This example is helpful because:

- an invitation to a gay wedding is about as clear an "ask" as any, as it often specifically requires a person to respond,
- an invitation to a gay wedding will often bring to the surface everything someone has ever believed, or thought they've believed, regarding homosexuality,
- and a response to a gay wedding invitation involves real people and real relationships, not abstract theories.

While many arguments could be made for attending or not attending a gay wedding—even among devout, Bible-believing Christians who hold to the belief that gay marriage isn't right, good or healthy for those getting married—a thoughtful discussion on this topic can be helpful. Some of these responses vary based on the relationships and beliefs of those who are doing the inviting and being invited, such as:

- whether or not attendance violates a person's conscience,
- whether or not attendance equates to approval,
- and whether or not attendance will significantly impact the relationship between those doing the inviting and those being invited.

Some additional considerations to take into account include:

- how God has come alongside us even when we've done things He hasn't wanted us to do,
- how coming alongside someone in celebration is significantly different from coming alongside while holding back tears,
- and how both tough love and genuine kindness can lead to the same result, depending on the situation.

While this chapter focuses on gay marriage as an example, it illustrates the very real dilemma Christians will face in their lives with those they love. The author trusts that God can guide us into the most loving approach if we will give the situation some time, some prayer, and some deep thought.

QUESTIONS FOR REFLECTION & DISCUSSION

Read 1 Corinthians 13:2 and 16:14. What should always guide our response to any issue, cultural or otherwise?

Read Ecclesiastes 3:1, 7 and James 1:19. What do these passages say about the issue of when to speak and when to stay silent? Have you ever been asked to respond to what you believe about the issue of homosexuality? If so, how do you feel you did in your response? What might you wish you had done better?

Read Romans 1:32 and Hebrews 13:5b. How might each of these passages guide someone into knowing whether or not to attend a gay wedding? Does attendance at a wedding necessarily equate to approval of that wedding? How would your answer to the previous question affect whether or not you might attend?

Read John 8:1-11, John 3:17, and Romans 5:8. How was Jesus able to let the woman who had committed adultery go free? What was He headed to do on her behalf to make her freedom possible? Although we can't die for someone's sins as Jesus did so they could be free, how might we *live* for them so they could be free? What did Christ do for us while we were still sinning?

Read Romans 2:4. To what can God's kindness eventually lead? What are some kindnesses we might extend to others that might lead to the same thing?

Have you ever been invited to attend a wedding of *any* kind where you didn't necessarily approve of the union, but you went anyway? If you did or didn't go, what factors played a role in your decision? How might those factors be helpful in regards to attending or not attending a gay wedding?

Have you ever been invited to attend a gay wedding? If so, what has been your response, and why? And whether you have been invited to a gay wedding or not, why is it so important to give your response some time, some prayer, and some deep thought?

Conclusion:

Why We All Need A Rainbow

———— ❖ ————

In which I share why the rainbow is a fitting sign, not only for the gay movement, but for all of us—because we're all in this together.

———— ❖ ————

Sometimes as Christians, we think that we're on the inside track with God. We think we're in His "in" group, and everyone else is on the "outside." We miss the fact that everyone is precious in God's sight— that we're all created in His image.

I realized this in a poignant way when I went to Israel for the first time in 1995. I was staying with a Muslim family on the West Bank, in a home where bullets, at some point in the past, had riddled the outside walls and the window panes of the room in which I was sleeping.

Here I was, an on-fire Christian visiting Israel for the first time, less than 10 days after I had quit my secular job to go into full-time ministry. I had come on a journey of faith, with God alone, and was living for a week with a family that I had only even *heard about* the morning I left home to go to the airport.

A friend of mine had arranged my lodging that same morning with a Muslim friend of his who ran the grocery store in our small town and who offered me a place to stay with his relatives there while I toured the country.

This Muslim family was exceedingly gracious and kind, treating me like royalty—even though they mentioned in passing on the day I arrived that if they ever met the American evangelist Billy Graham, they would kill him on the spot. (I decided that wasn't the time to mention that Mr. Graham is one of my living heroes of the faith, and that my wife and I had given his last name as the middle name to one of our children. There really is a time to speak and a time to stay silent!)

While this family was super hospitable, as kind as any family I had ever met, I still had this feeling inside me that because I was a Christian, I had a special "in" with God, and that they were somehow "outside" of that circle.

I do understand, theologically, that Christ *does* open a door for us to come to God, clean and forgiven, which *does* avail us of incredible blessings and benefits, including eternal life! But in terms of being *precious* in God's sight, we're all on the same level playing field.

One night, after coming home from visiting some of the Holy Sites in that Holy Land, it dawned on me: I was, in fact, a Gentile (as the Bible refers to anyone who is not Jewish), just the same as my Muslim hosts were Gentiles. That's when it struck me that I was no more of an "insider" with God than they were.

According to any orthodox Jew, I was more like this Muslim family than I was like most of the early Jewish followers of Jesus. God impressed it on my heart that day that the only difference between me and my Muslim hosts was that I had put my faith in Christ and my hosts had not—which is a difference that really does make all the difference in the world, both here in this world as well as in the next. Yet by my natural birth, I was just as much a Gentile as my hosts.

I suddenly felt a oneness with my host family that I had never felt before. I realized that I had been in the exact same boat as they were. It was only because of Christ's willingness to open the doors of God's kingdom to *everyone* that I, as a Gentile, had even been given a chance to enter into that kingdom.

PEOPLE ARE PEOPLE

I share this with you as you consider how to love God and love gays better. The truth is, it's not a matter of "us versus them," but of "we're all in this together."

In many ways, I feel as far removed from being gay as anyone who has never experienced same-sex attractions at all. It's like I am now "this," while they are still "that." But the truth is, we're *all* "that"—we're all in need of God's mercy and grace, because we've all sinned in one way or another.

And we all come back to God in the same way, too: through the love and forgiveness offered to us by Jesus Christ.

Romans 1 has some strong words of warning for those who have gone into homosexuality, among other things. But Romans 2 has some strong words of warning for everyone else:

"You, therefore, have no excuse, you who pass judgment on someone else, for at whatever point you judge the other, you are condemning yourself, because you who pass judgment do the same things... So when you, a mere man, pass judgment on them and yet do the same things, do you think you will escape God's judgment? Or do you show contempt for the riches of His kindness, tolerance and patience, not realizing that God's kindness leads you toward repentance?" (Romans 2:1, 3-4).

Throughout this book, I've tried to convey that people who struggle with same-sex attractions aren't much different from anyone else who struggles with any other kind of temptation.

We're *all* attracted to *something* that isn't good or healthy for us. We're *all* attracted to *something* which God tries to warn us against with His clearest and strongest possible "No." We're *all* in need of God's love, God's compassion, and God's grace, which He has so freely offered to each of us through Jesus Christ.

The author of the popular book series I mentioned earlier—the one who said that she always thought of one of the main heroes of her books as gay—responded to a tweet one day from a fan who wrote that she "couldn't see it."

This fan said she had read all the books in the series from cover to cover and didn't get from any of them that this important character was gay.

The author replied: "Maybe because gay people just look like... people?"

Wow! What a response! What a revelation! And how so completely true, on so many levels.

People *are* people. We *all* have things with which we struggle, and we *all* have things from which we need to be saved. None of us has a perfect moral scorecard. We really are "all in this together."

ROSE-COLORED GLASSES

We all need, as Noah and his family needed after the flood, a rainbow in the sky, a promise from God that He won't wipe us out with a flood ever again.

I was intrigued when I first started reading the Bible as an adult that as early as Chapter 6 of the first book, Genesis, we as people had already strayed so far from God's hopes and dreams for us that He was ready and willing to destroy everything He had created.

God found one person, however, who did what was right in His eyes, and because of even one person, God was willing to give us all another go.

God saved Noah and his family from His nearly all-out destruction, then made a promise afterward that He would never again destroy the earth with a flood. You know the story: God then put a rainbow in the clouds as a sign of that promise.

What I *didn't* realize until I was reading that story as an adult was *who* the sign was for. I always thought the rainbow was a sign for *us*, His sons and daughters on earth, to remind *us* that He would never again destroy the earth. But as I looked closer at the passage, I saw the rainbow was actually a sign for *Him*, a reminder to *Him* of the promise that He had made.

God said, "Whenever I bring clouds over the earth and the rainbow appears in the clouds, I will remember my covenant between Me and you and all living creatures of every kind. Never again will the waters become a flood to destroy all life" (Genesis 9:14-15).

This shifted my thinking on the rainbow. Instead of being a sign for me, it was a sign for Him. It struck me that the rainbow, for God, is like a pair of rose-colored glasses—God-sized glasses—through which He can view the earth in a fresh way.

I've had a pair of rose-colored sunglasses before. While I've had sunglasses of other colors—gray, blue, and brown—none of them seemed to enhance what I saw around me as much as those which were rose-colored.

Whenever I put them on, everything around me looked a little brighter, a little better. It was as if I had a whole new outlook on life—a whole new outlook on everything I saw.

After reading this passage about the rainbow from *God's* perspective, I could now imagine Him looking at me, and instead of seeing the *ugliness* of me—the things I had done which had marred my own image—He saw me in a new light.

I could imagine that to God, He saw me a little brighter, a little better.

When God looks at us through His rainbow, it's as if He's seeing us as He *originally* created us, the way He had hoped we would be from the beginning.

Then I thought about those in the gay movement who have chosen the rainbow as their symbol, who have stuck rainbow stickers on their cars, and who have flown rainbow flags over their homes. I couldn't help but think that perhaps, in God's eyes, it helps Him to see things in a different light, a light that reminds Him of His promises once again.

HE'S WITH ME

And isn't that what Jesus has done for us? When Jesus came to earth and died for our sins, He became our new rainbow, our new covenant.

When God looks at me now, He sees Jesus instead, not because I'm so much like Jesus (although I wish I were), but because Jesus stands in front of me and says, "He's with me."

When Jesus took my place on the cross, a place which I had rightly earned because of my various sins, God covered me with the forgiveness that Christ bought with His life.

When God looks at me, He sees Jesus instead. He sees an enhanced Eric, a glorified Eric, a sanctified Eric—Eric 2.0—because He sees me through His Jesus-colored glasses.

Like the woman caught in adultery, I, too, was caught in my sins. And like the woman caught in adultery, Jesus said that I, too, could go free because He had gone to the cross to pay for my sins, allowing me to live the life God had created me to live in the first place. And as I was going out to live that new life, Jesus said to me, just as He said to the woman caught in adultery, "Go and sin no more."

We all need a rainbow. We all need Someone who can save us from our sins. We're all in this boat together.

I don't know about you, but I, for one, am thankful that God put that rainbow in the sky. I can't think of a better sign or a more fitting flag to fly over my life, not as a symbol of pride, but as a reminder of God's promises that He's made.

I've even wondered, at times, could it be that God Himself inspired those in the gay movement to choose the rainbow as their symbol, as the sign they could display over their homes, their parades, and their lives?

Could it be that God Himself had inspired someone in the White House to light it up in all the colors of the rainbow on the day our Supreme Court legalized gay marriage all across the country?

Could it be that God Himself had inspired people to fly the flag of the rainbow over our embassies all around the world?

I don't know the answer. But if it were God who had inspired each of those things, I'd be grateful.

Whenever I see a rainbow now, it reminds me of God's incredible love for me. It reminds me of His amazing grace. It reminds me that we're all in this together.

Most of all, it reminds me that we all need a rainbow every now and then.

Thanks to Jesus, who sent His Holy Spirit to dwell within everyone who puts their faith in Him, we have such a Rainbow—everywhere we go.

Study Guide For The Conclusion

STUDY GUIDE FOR THE CONCLUSION: "WHY WE ALL NEED A RAINBOW"

CHAPTER SUMMARY

It's sometimes easy to think in terms of "us" and "them" regarding *any* topic in life, let alone this one. But the truth is, we're all in this together. The truth is:

- none of us has a perfect moral scorecard,
- we're all in need of God's mercy and grace,
- and we all come back to God in the exact same way: by receiving through faith the love and forgiveness that is offered to us by Jesus Christ.

Just as the rainbow was a sign in Noah's day, it's still a sign for us today of God's promise that He will never again destroy the world with a flood. The rainbow:

- is a sign *to us* of God's promise, so we can rest assured in it,
- is a sign *to God* of His promise, so He will be reminded of it,
- and perhaps even serves as God-sized, rose-colored glasses so when He sees us, He sees us as He originally created us—without sin—just as He sees those who have put their faith in Christ as being made righteous in His sight.

While God Himself is obviously the inspiration behind all the rainbows in the sky, the author wonders if perhaps God is also the inspiration behind all the other rainbows that we see all around us in the world, regardless of who or why people display them, so we all will look a little brighter in God's sight.

If that's the case, then we could all use a rainbow over our lives— every day! And thanks to Jesus, we have one.

QUESTIONS FOR REFLECTION & DISCUSSION

Read Romans 2:1-4. Why does the Apostle Paul say that we who judge others for certain sins do the same things ourselves? What is his point in Romans 2:1-4?

Read Genesis 6:9-14, 7:21-24 and 9:1-17. What was happening in the days of Noah that made God want to destroy everyone in the world? Why did God decide to spare Noah and his family?

Do you sometimes think of this issue in terms of "us" and "them"? What do you think about the statement: "we're all in this together"? Why would the author say we're all in this together, even if someone has never experienced or never acted upon a same-sex attraction?

What do you think of the statement: "Maybe because gay people just look like... people?"

What difference would it make if, instead of facing those involved in homosexuality head on, we walked alongside them, side-by-side, to help walk them out of it?

Why did God need to set a reminder in the sky to never destroy the world again with a flood? For whom did He put it there? How do you think the rainbow helps both God *and* us every time one appears in the sky?

How can Jesus serve as a "rainbow" over the lives of those who put their faith in Him?

While God is clearly the inspiration behind every rainbow that appears in the sky, is it possible He is also the inspiration behind every rainbow we see in the mass of rainbows all around us every day? If so, what purpose might He have in doing so? How might this thought change your view of rainbows every time you see one from now on?

Afterword:

10 Steps Toward Better Understanding

———— ◈ ————

In which I share some practical ideas to guide your discussions on this topic with those who are experiencing same-sex attractions.

———— ◈ ————

Now that you've read this book, you might be asking, "So what do I do now?"

I've written this guide to give you some ideas for how to discuss this topic with those who are experiencing same-sex attractions. This is how I discuss this topic with those I love.

I pray this guide will help to multiply whatever God has been able to do through me so He can do it through you, too. Together, I hope we can have a positive impact on as many people as possible—including those you love the most.

STEP 1) KNOW WHAT YOU BELIEVE AND WHY YOU BELIEVE IT.

Before discussing this topic, it's helpful to identify what you've already come to believe on this topic and why you've come to those beliefs. While your beliefs may change over time with further exploration, prayer, and discussion, this is a good starting point for having a conversation.

Here's what I believe about this topic and why I believe it. Feel free to use this list as it is or use it as a springboard to create your own list.

The question is this: "What do you truly believe about homosexuality—and why?"

- I believe homosexual acts are sins. Why? Because God has warned us against them in the Bible, clearly and strongly. (Romans 1:8-32; Leviticus 18:22, 20:13; 1 Corinthians 6:9-20)
- I believe homosexual temptations are not sins. Why? Because God says we all face temptations, just as Jesus did, yet those temptations do not define us. (1 Corinthians 10:13; Hebrews 4:14-16)
- I believe anyone can be redeemed and delivered from acting on their homosexual temptations ever again. Why? Because God is in the life-changing business—even regarding this issue. (1 Corinthians 6:11-12; 2 Corinthians 5:17; plus my own testimony and the testimony of many others)
- I believe those who truly desire to eventually marry someone of the opposite sex can do so with wonderful results. Why? Because when we delight ourselves in the Lord, He will give us the desire of our hearts. (Psalm 37:4-6; John 10:7-10; plus my own testimony and the testimony of many others)
- I believe God's ideal for marriage is husband and wife, committed for life. Why? Because God has intentionally wired us in a way to simultaneously fulfill our desire for intimacy and His desire for a world full of people—because He loves people! (Genesis 1:26-28; Genesis 2:18-25; Mark 10:2-9; John 3:14-18)
- I believe homosexual relationships are neither the first-best nor the second-best option for anyone, but, in the long run, are destructive and harmful to those involved, to others, and to God's purposes for which He gave us the gift of sex. Why? Because if you do something God says not to do, it won't go well for you. (Romans 1:24-32; Romans 3:23, 6:23; Deuteronomy 28:1-2, 15)
- I believe God loves us unconditionally, calls us to live our lives to the fullest, and empowers us to do so. Why? Because of the way Jesus forgave people, called them to live their lives to the fullest, and empowered them to do so. (John 8:1-11; 1 Corinthians 6:9-11; Romans 8:9-11)

- I believe God calls us to love one another unconditionally, treating one another as we would want to be treated. Why? Because Jesus loved us this way and called us to do the same. (Matthew 7:12; Matthew 22:34-40; Romans 5:6-8)

STEP 2) LEARN WHAT YOUR LOVED ONES BELIEVE AND WHY THEY BELIEVE IT.

- Ask your loved ones to tell you their stories as honestly as possible, truly listening to them with the goal of understanding—not just responding. (James 1:19-20; Proverbs 10:19, 18:2, 18:13)
- Listen to their hearts, not just their words, so you can hear what they're saying more fully and clearly (and possibly take less offense at any of their particular words). (Proverbs 20:5)
- Listen for valid needs they are wanting to fulfill. (Philippians 4:19)
- Listen for ways they are trying to fulfill those valid needs, whether those ways seem valid or invalid. (Proverbs 3:5-6)

STEP 3) SHARE WHAT YOU BELIEVE AND WHY YOU BELIEVE IT.

- Share, in love, the truths you've come to believe. (Ephesians 4:15)
- Share, in love, the Scriptures which support your beliefs, trusting that those Scriptures will come to life for those who hear them. (Hebrews 4:12)
- Share, in love, the story of the Corinthians in the Bible, my story, and the stories of others who embody what you believe. For starters: share this book or share my full story, *Fifty Shades of Grace*, written under my pen name Nicholas Deere; or Dennis Jernigan's story, *Sing Over Me;* or Jeff Konrad's story, *You Don't Have to be Gay;* or Christopher Yuan's story, *Out of a Far Country*. (1 Corinthians 6:9-11; John 20:30-31; John 21:25)

STEP 4) IDENTIFY POINTS OF AGREEMENT AND POINTS OF DISAGREEMENT.

- Identify points of agreement in each other's views, especially regarding valid needs, recognizing there is power in agreement. (Matthew 18:19)
- Identify points of disagreement in each other's views, especially regarding ways to meet those valid needs which might seem invalid to each of you, recognizing that even those who are mature sometimes hold differing views. (Philippians 3:15-16; Galatians 2:11)
- Identify possible harms which could come from meeting valid needs in ways that each of you might consider to be invalid—including harms to those involved, harms to others, and harms to the purposes for which God has given us His gift of sex. (1 Corinthians 6:18-20; Romans 1:27; Genesis 3:1-3)

STEP 5) EXPLORE IDEAS FOR MEETING VALID NEEDS IN VALID WAYS.

- Explore ideas for meeting valid needs in ways which are not sexual or romantic. (1 Samuel 18:1-4; Ruth 1:16-18; Proverbs 18:24; Acts 9:27, 11:25-26; 1 Timothy 1:2)
- Explore ways in which people can use their gifts and talents to honor God, yet not compromise their integrity. (Ephesians 2:10; Exodus 31:1-11; 1 Samuel 16:14-23; Genesis 4:21)

STEP 6) PRAY FOR ONE ANOTHER—FOR GOD'S WISDOM AND HEALING.

- Pray for each other, for God's wisdom to be revealed on this topic as fully as possible. (James 1:5-8)
- Pray for each other, to be healed of any hurts you may have received from anyone over this issue. (James 5:13-15)
- Ask for and receive forgiveness from each other for any hurts each of you may have inflicted on the other, whether

intentionally or unintentionally. (James 5:16; Ephesians 4:32; Colossians 3:12-14)

STEP 7) SET HEALTHY BOUNDARIES WITH EACH OTHER OUT OF MUTUAL HONOR AND RESPECT.

- Discuss ways in which each of you could truly honor and respect one another's deeply held beliefs. (Romans 12:10)
- Discuss limits or restraints which would be truly helpful for honoring and respecting one another's deeply held beliefs. (1 Corinthians 10:23-31)

STEP 8) LEAVE THE DOOR OPEN FOR FURTHER CONVERSATIONS—BUT DON'T NAG!

- Keep the door open to further conversations, realizing that prayerful insights and answers often come to us over time. (Romans 8:22-28; 12:18)
- Treat your conversations on this topic as holy and precious— because they are—not trivial or flippant. (Proverbs 21:19; Colossians 3:21; Proverbs 25:11; 27:15-16)
- When you do disagree, disagree with civility. (Proverbs 15:1-7; Luke 12:58; Romans 15:1-7; 2 Timothy 2:14)

STEP 9) ENJOY THOSE PARTS OF YOUR RELATIONSHIP WHICH YOU *CAN* ENJOY!

- Enjoy the gift of each other that God has given to you, regardless of your deeply held beliefs on this particular topic. (John 13:34-35)
- Let each other exercise their free will as God lets each of us exercise ours, all while honoring and respecting one another. (Galatians 5:13)

STEP 10) LET NOTHING SEPARATE YOU FROM YOUR LOVE FOR ONE ANOTHER—EVEN THIS TOPIC—JUST AS NOTHING CAN SEPARATE YOU FROM THE LOVE OF GOD.

- Remember that nothing can separate you from the love of God. (Romans 8:34-39)
- Commit to letting nothing separate you from those you love— even this topic. (Ruth 1:16-18)

About The Author

Described by *USA Today* as "a new breed of evangelist," Eric Elder is an author, speaker, and contemporary pianist. Eric is also an ordained pastor and the creator of *The Ranch*, a faith-boosting website at:

WWW.THERANCH.ORG

Also by Eric Elder:

Two Weeks With God
What God Says About Sex
Exodus: Lessons In Freedom
Jesus: Lessons In Love
Acts: Lessons In Faith
Nehemiah: Lessons In Rebuilding
Ephesians: Lessons In Grace
Israel: Lessons From The Holy Land
Israel For Kids: Lessons From The Holy Land
The Top 20 Passages In The Bible
Romans: Lessons In Renewing Your Mind
St. Nicholas: The Believer
San Nicolás: El Creyente (Spanish Edition)
Making The Most Of The Darkness
15 Tips For A Stronger Marriage
Fifty Shades Of Grace (under the pen name Nicholas Deere)
Water From My Well

To learn more, please visit:
WWW.INSPIRINGBOOKS.COM

To contact Eric Elder:
Eric is always glad to hear from his readers!
You can write to him anytime at: eric@theranch.org

77522049R00126

Made in the USA
San Bernardino, CA
24 May 2018